GODDESS POWER

Other Books by Dr. Don Parker

Schooling for What?
Schooling for Individual Excellence
SRA Reading Laboratory Series

Into the 21st Century with

GODDESS POWER

An interactive book
for women...and men

Don Parker, Ph.D.

Dynamic Publishing, Carmel CA, U.S.A.

Grateful acknowledgment is made for permission to reprint from the following:

Goddesses in Everywoman. Copyright © 1984 by Jean Shinoda Bolen. Reprinted by permission of Jean Shinoda Bolen.

The Once and Future Goddess. Copyright © 1989 Elinor W. Gadon. Reprinted by permission of HarperCollins Publishes, Inc.

Men Are From Mars, Women Are From Venus. Copyright © 1992 John Gray. Reprinted by permission of HarperCollins.

The Book Of Signs. Copyright © 1930 by Rudolf Koch. Reprinted by permission of Dover Publications.

"Powerful Men: Are They As Good In The Bedroom As They Are In The Boardroom?", copyright © Feb 1995 by *Cosmopolitan.* Reprinted by permission of Cosmopolitan.

"The Way To Be Surely, Surely Sexy" by JoAnna Nicholson. *Cosmopolitan*, February 1995. Reprinted by permission of JoAnna Nicholson and Cosmopolitan.

"Lovestyles" by Steven Prasinos and Bennett I. Tittler Journal of *Humanistic Psychology,* Vol. 24, No. 1, p. 175, copyright © Winter, 1984 by Sage Publications. Reprinted by permission of Sage Publications, Inc.

"Less Than Uplifting" by Margaret Carlson. Time, copyright © April 4, 1994 by Time. Reprinted by permission of Time, Inc.

Photography by Don H. Parker. Cover drawings by Fritzi Parker.

FIRST EDITION — Printed in the United States of America.

Publisher's Cataloging in Publication
(Prepared by Quality Books Inc.)

Parker, Don H.
    Goddess power / Don H. Parker.
    p. cm.
    Includes bibliographical references and index.
    ISBN 0-9648077-0-X

    1. Self-actualization (Psychology) 2. Women—Psychology. 3. Goddesses—Psychological aspects. 4. Mythology, Greek—Psychological aspects. 5. Sex role. I. Title.

BF637.S4P37 1996   158.1
                                    QBI95-20397

Dedication

*To the Goddesses in
you, and in every
woman, and to the
men who will come to
appreciate them.*

Contents

Contents (Cont'd)

Preface

Why, really, did I want to write this book? Because, at 83 years young, I have lived through enough marriages and relationships to realize that had I known and appreciated each of the wonderful Seven Goddesses in the make-up of each woman, their lives would have been more happy and fulfilled—and so would mine.

Still further, I wanted to join the increasing number of thoughtful people of both sexes who are now realizing that if we don't re-examine, and reactivate, the life-giving, life-nurturing female principle of Goddess Power our stay on Planet Earth will become shorter and shorter. "The Gaea (from Greek Gaia) Hypothesis" put forward by British scientist James Lovelock sees the Great Goddess Mother Earth as a living, breathing organism. Either we protect it, nourish it, or deal ourselves a slow death as we literally eat up and spit out her resources, not retaining them long enough to nurture the body-mind-spirit of the human race, or of each of us. I am deeply committed to the proposition that the more a woman knows about the power of her Seven Goddesses and the more men embrace the concept of Goddess Power—in relationships, marriage or in the workplace—the better chance we have not only for survival on Planet Earth but for a bright future.

But beyond all that, my own increasing appreciation for womankind pulls like a magnet to deepen my understanding of the feminine mystique.

Preparing for this book over the past ten years, I have made three pilgrimages to Greece to stand in the very presence of Goddess Power as once it was, and as it must return, down to date into the 21st Century. In addition, I have immersed myself in over five dozen books and scanned dozens more—books by and about women—delving into women's history as far back as 30,000 years. And I have called for help on fellow professional psychologists. However, my most valuable assistance and encouragement has come from the 203 women with whom I have discussed, often in depth, how a woman can best learn about her own Goddess Power, the status of women today and how things will be for women and men as we move into the 21st Century.

Women approaching the millennium are moving into uncharted waters and taking men with them—like it or not. But Goddess Power is not about power *over*, but power *with*. It's about woman-man partnership. It's the dawn of a new day. Up through 30,000 years of history, women gained respect and power as producers and nurturers of life. They earned Goddess Power. Men held women in awe.

But as men became aware that they had something to do with creating life, they set about the biggest power grab in history. They robbed women of their power. Now, the pendulum swings back; Goddess Power is reasserting itself.

Why draw on the mythology of the Seven Goddesses? Because humans have always felt the need to explain the world. Mythology is the story we tell each other how the world works, and to feel a link with something beyond "reality." A personal mythology is what we tell ourselves about how *our* life works. Let your Seven Goddesses help you to build a solid and satisfying personal mythology for yourself.

The Seven Goddesses open up new windows for the universe of a woman. Instead of a shapeless glob of notions about herself, getting to know the Seven Goddesses within her—and within every woman—she finds a structure based on her archetypal consciousness of the very nature of women as she has developed up through the centuries. Here is a road map back to her future—the future of all of us.

In her book, *Who Stole Feminism?* Christina Hoff Sommers is greatly concerned that American feminism is currently being dominated by a relatively small minority of women who, instead of helping the women's movement, is creating a backlash to the backlash. She cites courses in women's studies and other activities that are teaching young women to believe that "women are virtually under siege" and that they "seek recruits to wage their side of" what they see as a "gender war." It is hoped that this book will help to level the field for all players—including the gender warriors.

Will the upsurge of Goddess Power rob men of their present power *over* position? In the view of some, yes. But deep in the perception of the intelligent, thinking male is the vision of not only sharing the stresses of life, but finding life easier and more fulfilling as women are more and more empowered to "hold up their end of the sky." And they will do it without losing their ineluctable femininity!

Acknowledgements

I shall be forever in debt to Jean Shinoda Bolen, M.D., a psychiatrist, for identifying and personalizing the Seven Goddesses that appear in her landmark book, *Goddesses In Everywoman*, My own study of the hundreds of goddesses throughout the recorded history of cultures around the world, has only served to heighten my appreciation for her penetrating research in connecting the particular seven mythological goddesses she has chosen with the lives of women today.

Dr. Elinor Gadon's richly illustrated *The Onceand Future Goddess* has brought a treasure of germinal insights into women's sexuality in many cultures and its implication for richer woman-man experiences.

Moving successfully into the 21st Century will, in no small measure, depend on Riane Eisler's concept of an active man-woman partnership. In her book, *The Chalice and the Blade,* she argues eloquently for women and men as equal partners, adding useful dimensions to my thinking. Ashley Montagu has called her work "The most important book since Darwin's *Origin of the Species.* Indeed, making partnership work may require men to become a "new species" and women to help them toward an almost "genetic change."

In this book, I have attempted to extend the meaningfulness of their work to the countless women and men who are subconsciously crying out for a deeper understanding of what makes them desire and do the things they do, especially in their relationships with each other. And, fervently, I hope that womankind can bring to men a working understanding of the feminine principles—nurturing, feeling, conserving—

in a living relationship with Gaia, the Mother Earth Goddess, in time to save our cosmic home—Planet Earth.

For a photographer, working with a professional model is a peak experience. And so it has been for me, capturing through the lens, the beauty and the range of professional skills Jan Dymke Quaglia brought to the project as she acted out the multitudinous characteristics of the Seven Goddesses. One could not ask for a more sincere effort on the part of a model to understand and project the range of goddess qualities you will literally experience *with* her.

And no one could appreciate more than I, as both author and photographer, the sweat, and, yes, at times the tears as she posed and re-posed, time after time, to "get it right" so the message would penetrate deeply into *your* body-mind-spirit.

In addition to the work of Jean Shinoda Bolen and Riane Eisler, many other researchers and writers have contributed to my understanding of the goddesses concept and the mythologies of many cultures. No acknowledgement would be complete without a special tribute to Marija Gimbutas and her ground-breaking *The Language of the Goddesses* based on her own archaeological findings. In the *Woman's Encyclopedia of Myths and Secrets*, Barbara Walker spread before me a panoply of goddesses from around the world.

My greatest debt is to each of the 203 women, aged 18-83, who have taken time to profile their Goddess Characteristics Chart, respond to Goddess pictures, discuss their feelings about the Goddess concept and the implications for their lives. As "fellow researchers," they have given to me of their Goddess Power. Among those who have read and made valuable comments on the manuscript-in-work, I give special appreciation to La Vonne Rae Andrews, Judith Bergfors,

Betty Byron, Marsha Coupé, Ria Helton, Zephyr Halfen, Ina Hillebrant, Nancy Jungerman, Olivia Morgan, Terry Nash and my wife, Fritzi. Mary Scott was especially helpful in elaborating the Goddess Checklist "Digging Deeper." Jeseph De Alejandro, Paul Hensler and Stuart Miller have given valuable male input. Especially helpful have been the views of Dr. Stanley Krippner, Professor of Psychology, Saybrook Institute, world lecturer and co-author of *Personal Mythology*.

Yvonne Simons brought to the final ms. project not only her organized mind but the heart of a woman dedicated to seeing the Seven Goddesses take their rightful places in a world so in need of them.

Kelly Bernard, longtime friend and talented teacher of English, offered his services as proofreader of the final manuscript, as well as creator of the index. Thank you, Kelly!

I would have been lost in the maze of today's computerized graphics, pre-press and printing techniques without the willingly applied knowledge and expertise of David Lees to guide the manuscript into the real-life book you now hold in your hands.

As a man, I acknowledge my share of causing women pain through marriages and relationships. Hopefully, this book will help other men—and women—to move their dialogues to higher grounds of loving partnership.

Introduction

What's in the book? Forty-four short, exciting, door-opening chapters to bring the understanding and energy of Goddess Power to women—and men—as we move into the 21st Century.

Bringing to the service of you, my reader, is the publication of my work in helping people of all ages learn how to read and think more clearly has reached over 61,000,000 students in 62 countries around the world. This multilevel learning process, step by step, level by level, *interactive media design* has been incorporated in this work.

In the mode of the new *interactive media,* you will not "just sit there" passively reading as with the usual book. Instead, you will be almost *living* with your Seven Goddesses as your mind puts words and pictures together, their messages penetrating deeply into your consciousness. Be prepared for many delightful "Ah-ha!" experiences as sudden insights reveal the surprising range and richness which living, loving and working with the Seven Goddesses will now bring into your life. And the Goddess Games! Play them all. I have created each one as a mirror for you to hold up and see yourself—all the wonderful things you are—and perhaps some of the less wonderful you'd like to change toward the real *you* you are discovering.

First, you will meet each of your Seven Goddesses. Then, in Goddess Game One, you will take pencil (or pen) in hand and check off your own Goddess Characteristic Chart. In Game Two you will begin to "Know Your Goddesses Even Better." Both of these were developed from a searching out of over 800 different characteristics embodied in the seven mythological goddesses chosen here to guide you.

The problem of capturing the essence of each goddess in a brief but comprehensive fashion was a tough one. To solve it, I consulted with professional psychologists to reduce the 800 items to ten for each goddess. Along the way, the judgment of 203 women became my richest source of decision making. The process required over a year. Now, in only a few minutes, you can start your journey into Goddess Power.

Throughout the rest of the book you will elaborate your understanding of each Goddess, how they relate to you and how each one can best serve your needs. Here, too, you will dig back into the exciting mythology and history of each one and how the mystery, the power and the guidance of each one will translate into your real, everyday life.

Why so many photographs? To dramatize how *one woman (and you!)* can put herself into each of the Seven Goddesses. Also to make the book easier to get into and save time for busy women—and men. And wasn't it an ancient Greek who said, "A picture is worth a thousand words?"

And, again, the Goddess Games. Don't miss a one of them. Each is designed to add a new dimension to your understanding. And they're fun!

Along the way you will explore the many meanings of love, and how to express them. You will find ways of dealing with disappointments.

Many of my women advisors have told me, "Why don't you suggest to your readers a *Goddess Party?* And so I have, at the very end of the book, for you to consider the fun and the excitement of sharing your learnings and how you are going to use them as you move into the 21st Century. And think what can happen if your party includes men!

Consider...

What would you like to get out of this book?

Level One:

> A good read about the Goddesses, and how they got that way? Read and enjoy!

Level Two:

> Make friends with your Seven Goddesses? Play some GODDESS GAMES as you read along. Have fun!

Level Three:

> Deeply desire to discover your authentic self? Find more ways of expressing the *real* you? *Experience* "Getting There With Goddess Power? Then do it all, page by page, step by enriching step. You'll find that getting into the 21st Century with Goddess Power can be excit ing, worth every minute of your time and fun!

1. Every Woman Has It: Goddess Power

Discover your Goddess Power! Find not only where you want to go, but also how to make your very best entrance on the stage of the 21st Century But why wait? Begin now! Your Goddess Power is unique, one of a kind. This book will help you find it and use it to get where you want to go. First you will learn how to tap into the wisdom of the Seven Goddesses within you—within every woman—and you will clarify your goals, envision your best options for attaining them, and enrich your body-mind-spirit.

Unleash the Goddess Power within *you* by discovering which Goddess rules your head, your heart, your dreams, your destiny. How can you take what the world offers you at every turn? How can you give back to the world all the wonderful things you have to offer?

Get to know the Goddesses in you—all seven of them. They're wonderful! They have come down through hundreds of years of Greek and Roman mythology. Today, they are alive, well and living in YOU. Love them all. Each one can help you in your work-life, your play-life, your love-life and in your parenting-life (if you so choose). To know your Goddesses is to know yourself. And you will have a new self-image!

There's *Artemis,* Goddess of Nature, Competitor, Sister. She can help you through a lot.

Then there's *Athena,* Goddess of Wisdom. Her help is indispensable.

Hestia, Goddess of Hearth and Temple will enrich your

inner life.

Hera, Goddess of Marriage, may or may not beckon strongly. But if you need her, she is there to help you fulfill that destiny.

Demeter, Goddess of Grain, Nurturer, Mother will lead your journey to the depths of womanhood.

Goddess *Persephone* is Springtime. She is fun. She is soft and pliable. She will be your playmate. Play!

And now, *Aphrodite,* Goddess of Love, Beauty and Creativity. She will help you find and express your special way of loving, your own unique beauty and open up your creativity as you move through your days and years. "Creative, me?" Yes, you, from the way you arrange flowers in a vase to all your ways of loving other living things—including men!

Now you have met all your Goddesses, and they are *you.* As we go along, you'll get better acquainted with their ancient truths, and how each one lives in you today.

Your combination, or "constellation" of Seven Goddesses is unique to you alone. Nothing on earth or in the heavens is just like you. No other woman in the world has your Goddess "mix," or the way you express each one.

Your Seven Goddesses are inseparable, a constellation of stars. Yet each Goddess is a star in her own right. You can beckon each to center stage at different seasons of your life. Even at different times of each day. And as you commune more deeply with each of your Goddesses, you reach up toward your highest self and your greatest joy.

What is Goddess Power? First of all, it's something every woman has because she is a woman. Learning the nature of it, and how to *use* YOUR Goddess Power is why you are reading this book.

You can discover and learn how to use your Goddess Power from the secret history of women, the history of half of the world's population that has been kept hidden for over five-thousand years.

When you learn how to use your Goddess Power, you will discover new options and explore new roles.

When you learn how to use your Goddess Power, you will, if you choose, be able to move with the women's movement toward a partnership society and world peace, without fear of losing your femininity.

How do I know this? Because the 203 women with whom I have worked to produce this book, ages 16-83, many probably like yourself, have encouraged me to pass this message on to you. Whether you see yourself more of a "Traditional Woman," or as one moving toward being "New Woman," you can learn to *use your Goddess Power*. You will discover a new you and a new way of relating to others—especially with men.

What has kept—is keeping—women from using their Goddess Power? Two things: Women's own self-image, and men. Not all men, but too many men still seek to "keep woman in her place."

As you move through this book, you will discover new ways of *being* and new understandings of your own Goddess Power. Your new Goddess Power will encourage you to begin relating to men in new ways. You will need courage to risk. But by knowing the hidden history of women you will gain confidence that you can help a man to see where you are coming from and how you can both find your best selves in a partnership relationship that can not damage but only enhance his masculinity and your femininity. He can be more of a man, you can be more of a woman.

Perhaps even more importantly, you can help men, even *one* man, to embrace and apply the conserving feminine principle, turning from masculine macho destructive tendencies toward more planet-conserving behavior which seems to come more naturally to women. If men are, indeed, "from Mars," as John Gray would put it, women can help them to leave their Mars-like behavior on that planet and join the women "from Venus" on Planet Earth.

There are growing signs that this planet-saving principle is at work in the book, *Lifting the Veil: The Feminine Face of Science* by Linda Jean Shepherd. Her work is reviewed in the September, 1994 *Brain/Mind* newsletter noting that she "...explores the ways in which the theories and practices of science have been altered by the rise of women in its ranks." She sees the rise of a science based increasingly on "female" traits like nurturance, feeling, intuition, and cooperation.

Together, we'll be looking back down the centuries to discuss the sources of Goddess Power; how they got it, how they lost it. And, how they are regaining it. That's what this book is all about: Helping you, as an individual woman, to claim your own Goddess Power and to help men understand that only by having power *with,* instead of power *over* women, can our Planet Earth and its peoples survive.

To literally put your feet into the shoes of each of the Seven Goddesses, play Goddess Game One and respond to the pictures in Goddess Game Two, coming later in this book. Now you will start to bring the Seven Goddesses out of mythology into real life, *your* life. As you move through the pages, a range of Goddess Games and photographic scenarios will put you more deeply in touch with the characteristics of each Goddess. Even more importantly, you will increasingly experience *being* each one. You will "try them on for size," walk among them, feel their presence. Let all seven of your Goddesses into the depths of your subconscious mind to nurture a growing spirituality and your Oneness with all of Creation.

Along the way back to a civilization based more on feminine (Goddess) principles, we'll look at the pitfalls and how to smooth the journey. For example: What are men's fears that have created the backlash to the Women's Movement? How can you gently use your Goddess Power in healing the stand-off? Are men and women really different? How can we learn to respect our true differences and turn them into a powerhouse to fill both our needs as man, woman, and of society's big picture? How can you help us, we men, to become aware of the many kinds of love each of us— men and women— needs to nurture self-esteem and give back in kind? How can each of us learn to give a little and get back a bounty of love?

The most exciting thing you will be doing as you move through this book will be looking at your Seven Goddesses not only as individual sources of power, but becoming aware of the unique, one-of-a-kind constellation of *your* Seven Goddesses, the way the characteristics of each Goddess begin to cluster into a design, a grouping that becomes more meaningful as you look at it. Think how the constellation of seven stars has become our "Big Dipper." And, consider how the two pointers aim constantly at the North Star. In like manner, your own Goddess constellation can indicate a direction for you to follow. Your own "Star Trek" *into the 21st Century with Goddess Power.*

A woman
is not born,
but rather
becomes,
a woman.

Simone De Beauvoir
France, 1908-1986

2. My Journey Toward The Goddesses

You may be wondering why I, a man, have presumed to write a book for and about women. Even more brash, about how women can learn to know what they want, and how to get it! Why? Because the female of the species is no different than the male in their need to "know thyself" and make the most of it. And, for me, the feminine gender is far more interesting to work with and write about than my own kind.

So this is a book for you, a woman. But it might also turn out to be a book for men, too! Wouldn't you like to help him learn more about you—about all those wonderful Goddesses within you?

And think of the big picture. As men become more aware of, and begin to appreciate, the power of the Seven Goddesses within you, the way opens for creating a more sustainable lifestyle for Planet Earth. Woman was always the conservator and under the guidance of the Great Goddess Mother, Gaia, she will show man how to stop overpopulating the Planet and how man has to stop wantonly spending our natural resources on land, sea, and air.

Evidence of woman's influence is already on the upswing. A woman, Geraldine Ferraro, was selected as a Vice Presidential running mate. Increasingly, we see women in both houses of Congress. Women have become State Governors. Women judges now serve from the Supreme Court on down. Woman Cabinet Members, and increasingly, Presidents' "First Ladies" are making their thoughts heard and respected. And more and more, in the corporate world, women are bringing their different and longer range perspectives that may yet save the Planet.

Out of a dawning New Age, there is still hope. Marilyn Ferguson, publisher of *Brain/Mind, a Bulletin of Breakthroughs*, puts it this way:

> "THE NEW WORLD that's dancing in the
> night can only be realized by us
> personally in our interaction with others.
> It can't be designed, legislated, or
> ordained by institutions.
>
> The new age that has been hovering over
> us for a very long time has nothing to do
> with the calendar and everything to do with
> being awake, and we have heard it speaking
> all our lives:
>
> "Carpe diem, seize the day." "Go for broke."
> "Walk your talk." "Try your wings." "Do unto
> others..."
>
> "It's time."

My own need for better understanding woman, underscored by my attempts (or lack of attempts!) to understand the psychophysiology of womankind, is a glaring example. Over the years, I have been married more than once and experimented in various living-with arrangements, all of which have come to a dead end. Now, very late in the game, I have a wonderful relationship with Fritzi, my wife of fifteen years. And my increasing understanding of the Goddesses has helped me to appreciate her own unique constellation of the seven archetypical Goddesses—the *real* Fritzi with her own special needs and wants—and reap the daily give-and-take rewards of a truly compatible loving-living man-woman companionship. Disagree at times? Of course! But she knows when to temper the power of certain of her Goddesses, while I, at the same time, understand what she needs from me, and give more of myself in that direction. And vice-versa.

Every day, I feel more fortunate to be side-by-side with Fritzi. However, I regret deeply that I did not have even a smattering of knowledge, much less an understanding, of the Goddesses and the part they played in the needs and wants of the women in my past marriages and relationships. While that may not have kept us together, such knowledge and understanding might have at least made our times together more satisfying to both, and our parting less traumatic. Most importantly, with such Goddess awareness our early attempts at relating may have been seen by both of us as not destined for compatibility.

You can see now that this book is dedicated to heightening your self-understanding, enhancing your self-image and envisioning the many options for expressing *your* unique constellation of Goddesses.

Do you know the best parts of yourself, the characteristics that can make the most of *you*? In this increasingly complex and demanding world, do you know the attitudes and behavioral patterns that can keep you from being all you can be? Check it out with your seven Goddesses. Whether you are 17 or 75+, the Goddess Characteristics Chart on Page 21 will be your guide. *Claim the Goddess Power that is rightfully yours!*

Your seven Goddesses—the Goddesses in you and in

every other woman, can help you build on your best qualities and to put your best foot forward. And knowing your least bountiful characteristics can show you how to lighten up or eliminate ways you think and act that may be getting in your way toward being all that you can be. So let your seven wise Goddesses show you the way you see yourself, the way other women see you, and the way men see and relate to you.

As a psychologist, I have devoted my past forty-five years to developing a system of learning to help people improve their abilities to think, learn and deal with personal and social problems. These men, women and children have come from all walks of life and from many races and cultures on all six continents around the world. They have been amazed at how they have been able to tap into their real, in-born learning power, even as I was when I first began the exciting experiments in 1950. I did not seek to apply multilevel learning to personal-social development. But a funny thing happened to my students on the way to simply learning how to read and think more clearly: improved self-image. People began to feel better about themselves. They gained "I can" confidence. And this led to progress in their learning abilities far beyond their—and my, fondest expectations. Early on, in my personal work with over six thousand people of all ages, they'd begin telling me, even after just weeks of multilevel learning, "I didn't realize I could learn like that!" or "Wow, I'm not afraid to tackle the harder stuff now." And things like, "I didn't realize there was so much to this business of thinking and learning." They got insights, too. They began to learn and appreciate how their own learning-machinery and behavior works: "I can begin to understand why I do things like that. And to understand why others do, too," they were telling me. Here was an unexpected breakthrough in my work: the development of personal-social intelligence.

As the work extended through all the years and to thousands—then to over 61,000,000 students in 62 different cultures and countries around the world, I began to realize two things: *One*, people of both sexes and all ages want to learn what it is that they really want. *Two*, they want to learn how to get it. These two needs to learn are as important for women as they are for men. But the opportunity for learning and doing something about what they have learned has been largely denied to women until the coming of the Women's Movement. In this book, you will be applying multilevel learning—step by step, level by level—to travel as fast and as far as your learning rate and capacity will take you toward the goals you see opening up before you. *Trust your vision!*

Trust Your Vision — the way

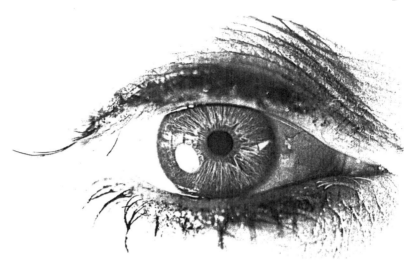

Achievers visualize goals. They image what they want. Visualize the way you want to be, then move toward that goal.

"But my goals are so fuzzy," you say, "and they seem so far away."

Yes, and often the more worthwhile, the fuzzier they at first appear. But as you move toward the distant goal, it becomes less fuzzy, more clear.

you are — the way you can be!

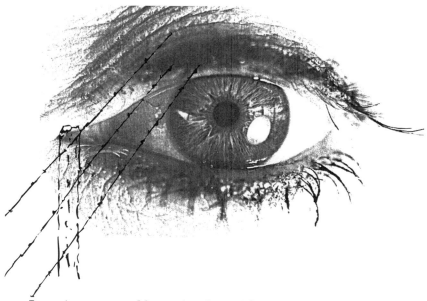

Imagine yourself out in the wide open spaces, standing near a row of fence posts stretching off into the distance. You can barely see the one way out there, perhaps a mile away. Now look at the one right next to you. How clearly you can see it. If your goal is to reach out and touch it, you can do it. You can observe its height, its thickness, the kind of wood its made of, how the wire is fastened to it. You can easily achieve your nearby goal.

As you look down the fence line, each post is less and less clear. But do you stand there moaning that you can't see the one way out there clearly. No, you start walking, start moving toward your goal and as you come near each post, it becomes as clearly visible as the first one. So start moving toward your goal, no matter how fuzzy, and the closer you approach it, the more clearly you can image it—and the stronger the image, the more incentive you will have to keep moving toward it. *Trust your vision*, THEN GO FOR IT!

Let your Goddesses guide you.

3. Your Own Goddess Characteristics

"Are there *really* seven goddesses in me?" you ask. Yes, and in every woman. In fact, there is a book entitled *The Goddesses in Everywoman,* by Dr. Jean Shinoda Bolen, a San Francisco psychiatrist.[*]

And do men know about this?

Yes, in a way, and they need some of all of them, each one in a different proportion. What's more, the kind of man attracted to you will depend on the goddesses you put "out front" most of the time.

And what about a career?

The career and life-style you choose, the options you choose and the roles you play follow your natural goddess characteristics.

Do I have to go along with all my goddesses just because they are there—just as they are, even if I don't like some of them?

No, not at all. You can't change innate characteristics, or temperament, as the psychologists call it, but you *can* change the way you express them.

---

[*] Published by Harper & Row, San Francisco, 1984. Available in bookstores: hardcover and soft cover, or from the publisher.

*Don't compromise yourself.
you are all you've got.*

–Janis Joplin–(1943-1970)
American Singer

This woman expresses feelings that sparked the women's movement in the early 60's

- *caught up in a power struggle*

  - *needing self-expression beyond "housewife"*

    - *aiming to be "all the woman she can be"*

There have always been women like this, calling on their Artemis-Athena strengths to overcome obstacles that "even a man" would find difficult. In the 50's, such women were rare. In the 60's, the hippie movement released more individuality for both women and men. The 70's found women surging ahead in this new break for individual freedom of choice and expression and the full-fledged women's movement was born. Now, well into the 80's and 90's, some women are having second thoughts. Have we, have I, been moving too fast and losing some of the very values we have been fighting for—a caring, nurturing better world? Are we losing, too, the feminine mystique?

Are you one of those who have adopted what traditionally have been considered "male tactics"—aggressiveness, single-mindedness, over-competitiveness? Then you are calling almost exclusively on your Goddesses Artemis and Athena. Do you sometimes long for softer feelings? Do you sometimes wish to express more of the characteristics of Hestia (spirituality), Hera (wifely companionship), Demeter (mothering, caring), Persephone (playfulness), Aphrodite (sexuality, creativity)?

Naturally, you feel the need for self-control in order to

draw on the strengths of your Artemis-Athena. But why not try opening up your body-mind-spirit to the other goddesses within you? Try giving them a little time in your life, if not prime time, then *some* time. In doing so, you will find life becoming more rewarding not only in happiness, but in moving toward your financial and security goals as well. One goddess can spark another, spreading creativity into your worklife and freeing up your lifestyle. Artemis-Athenas often get locked into—as Admiral Farragut put it—"damn the torpedoes, full speed ahead." There may be better ways.

Today, more and more women are poking their heads up through the fog of ignorance about themselves and about the world in general into the sunlight of, for them, a new world. For the first time, they are discovering new options. They are finding new choices. So many, in fact, that they are becoming confused as to what they really want, what best suits their real nature as a person and as a woman. As women look around at all the new life-styles, love-styles, work-styles and play-styles now opening up to them, questions begin to cry out for answers: "What do I really want?" "What suits my real nature as a person and as a woman—the real me?" And finding the answer leads to, "Now that I know what I want, how do I get it?"

Which goddesses do men like most?

It depends on the man, as you will see later. But first off, it's important that you know *your* goddess characteristics so you'll know what you've got to offer a man, a career, children and society in general.

The Goddesses within you, all seven of them, will help you find out what you really want and how to go about getting it. To know your Goddesses is to know yourself. Mythology will help.

Mythology is a story we tell each other about how the world works. According to Joseph Campbell who has now brought mythology into mainstream thinking, mythology is a set of beliefs that tries to explain why things happen and how they happen. In the study of the mythological gods and goddesses of ancient Greece and Rome, as well as deities down through the ages, we discover various belief systems and archetypes—personality patterns that seem inherent in the human race.

At the conclusion of a workshop conducted by Dr. Stanley Krippner at Esalen Institute in Big Sur, I asked him "What's the main difference in the concept of mythology as set forth by Joseph Campbell and the theme of your workshop on "A Personal Mythology?"

"It's really very simple," he replied. "While *general mythology* is the story we tell each other about how the world works, a *personal mythology* is the story we tell ourselves about how our *own* life works."

"Ah, so! I can see now why the sub-title of your recent book, *Personal Mythology*, is The Psychology of Your Evolving Self."

Your seven Goddesses will help you develop your own personal mythology. Knowing your seven Goddesses will help to heighten your self-understanding, enhance your self-image and envision options for the Goddess constellation within you.

How to begin? By turning now to the next page and doing the checklist under each one. *The few minutes you spend right now, before you go any further, will set the stage for your full use of this book toward your very best self.* Now, enjoy GODDESS GAME ONE and GODDESS GAME TWO.

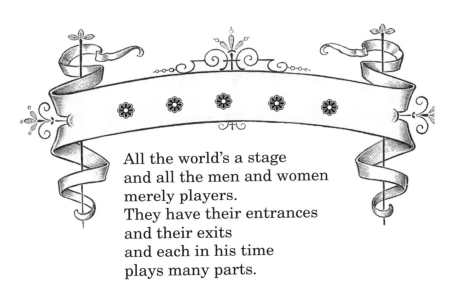

All the world's a stage
and all the men and women
merely players.
They have their entrances
and their exits
and each in his time
plays many parts.

–Shakespeare

"Goddess Characteristics": A Checklist. Name_____ Date_____

My age is _____ years. I am:

( ) a woman, describing myself

( ) a man describing ( ) a woman friend

( ) wife

( ) other _____

Directions For Women: Go down the list of all items for all 7 Goddesses and make a check mark in the column after each item that describes you as you are now. If an item does not apply, make no mark.

Directions For Men: have in mind a particular woman and follow directions above, checking to describe the way *you see her now.*

The Goddess Artemis

	√
feels equal to men	
affiliate of women	
strong sense of identity	
activist	
strongly felt causes	
nature lover	
assertive	
independent	
athletic	
men not needed	

The Goddess Athena

men as colleagues	
high achiever	
mature strategist	
cool under fire	
priority: own needs	
authoritative	
confident	
interest in world affairs	
physically active	
chaste	

The Goddess Hestia

spiritual	
non-assertive	
no sense of pressure	
quiet, introspective	
domestic	
orderly housekeeper	
inner centeredness	
loves rituals	
"old soul" presence	
excellent counselor	

- **Tear-out copy in back of book.**
- **Permission to photocopy for personal, non-commercial use hereby granted.**

Copyright © 1985 by Don H. Parker

The Goddess Hera

	√
marriage first, career 2nd	
wife first, mother 2nd	
personal friendships, 2nd	
seeks status symbol life	
heroic in support of mate	
blind to mate's defects	
jealous	
watchful	
radiant when happy	
shrew when betrayed	

The Goddess Demeter

loving	
motherhood paramount	
loves pregnancies	
enjoys serving others	
patient, persevering	
generous	
solid, dependable	
volunteering	
not "ambitious"	
"feminine" jobs	

The Goddess Persephone

extremely feminine	
compliant in nature	
can be "sex-kitten"	
adapts to wishes of others	
likes to be sheltered	
lacks direction	
difficulty following through	
rebellious	
manipulative	
dream oriented	

The Goddess Aphrodite

sensual, passionate	
unconventional	
creative, enthusiastic	
need variety in work	
need variety in men	
"here and now" attitude	
art, music, dance, poetry	
lover of laughter	
wide circle of friends	
not possessive, jealous	

For a closer look...Women: Look over the items under each Goddess again. Are there some characteristics you'd rather have less of? Then draw a line through that item. Like to have some additional qualities you do not now have? Draw a circle around those items. Now look at your "picture." **Men:** Do the same for the woman in your mind, describing how you would like her to be. Now look at her "picture."

Know your goddesses even better.

Who looks like whom?
Who says what?

First, look at the picture of each goddess,

Now look at picture No. 1. What are the chief goddess characteristics of this woman? With which goddess does she most closely identify? Write her name under the picture.

Next, put yourself in her place. Ask yourself: "What is she (am I) thinking right now?" Briefly write it underneath.

Artemis

Athena

Hestia

Hera

Demeter

Persephone

Aphrodite

1. _____
     Goddess

I am thinking _____
_____
_____

2. _____
     Goddess

I am thinking _____
_____
_____

3. _____
     Goddess

I am thinking _____
_____
_____

EDGAR GREGERSEN

Sexu

4. _____
     Goddess

I am thinking _____
_____
_____

5. _____
     Goddess

I am thinking _____
_____
_____

6. _____
     Goddess

I am thinking _____
_____
_____

7. _____
     Goddess

I am thinking _____
_____
_____

4. Now What?

So you've put down a baseline—checked off your characteristics under each of the seven goddesses, found your "heavy" ones and your "light" ones. What follows now is an introduction to each goddess. After that, a "paper movie" of pictures and words unfolds to portray many of the options and roles in which today's woman lives and breathes and has her being.

As you move through the various scenarios, you will get a number of different feelings. Some will strike you in the gut—that's me! That's what I should be doing! Others will turn you completely off—Ugh! What woman would want to do that? Still others will suggest combinations of options and roles and new kinds of interests, activities and even new careers to pursue. Some of these will have never entered your consciousness before: New windows to look through; new doors to open! Finally, there will be those to which you give a nod of recognition: Ah-h so! That's me, and I like it exactly where I am.

As you are learning, this inter-active, self-help book will give you the tools to fashion the woman you really want to be. So from here on in, take time to even more fully enjoy, to literally *live* in each of the situations and scenarios. Feel them in your gut. Go for identifying and knowing more about all those wonderful goddesses within you. See which ones you want to make friends with, get more power from. Find out which you'd like to know a little less, to free yourself from their power over you.

This book is designed to present you with alternatives, give you options, suggest new roles. And always, you will be asking the question: Men? How much do I need a man in what I really want to do, the kind of woman I want to be?

I am not about to suggest that because your Goddess chart profile is "long" here and "short" there, you are only capable of doing this or that. What I can tell you is that your own Goddess-mix is so different from any other of the two-and-half billion women on Earth that only *you* can know how to interpret and act on what you see in your Goddess characteristic profile chart.

By studying your Goddess chart on page 21 and considering carefully the options and roles pictured throughout this book, you will find opening out before you a map of the territory for your own unique lifetrip. And you will have an increasing sense of the strength of your various needs, drives and wants—the things that really turn you on, or off—and the Goddesses you will need to call on to achieve a goal or avoid a hazard.

Consider, for example, Artemis, Goddess of the Hunt, Competitor, Sister. Do you need more of her assertiveness, or is that quality now getting in the way of friendships—especially male relationships?

Athena, Goddess of Wisdom and Crafts, could thrust you into singleminded pursuit of a career—and the risk of losing satisfying experiences your other Goddesses could give you. Are you ready to pay the price?

Do you actually long to pull back from "the roaring traffic's boom"—the rush to acquire that new Mercedes?

Would you seek more wholeness in the quiet pursuits of Hestia, Goddess of Hearth and Temple? Do you experience your strongest satisfaction as a homemaker and keeper of the inner flame of your spiritual temple—and of those about you?

Does Hera, Goddess of Marriage, beckon most strongly of all? Does your self-esteem require, above all else, a husband? Is "wife" the career you long for? Do you find difficulty in understanding why some women prefer to leave the "r" out of "Mrs."—the "r" standing for the "rope" that may never be long enough? Or do you find the "r" a comfortable assurance of "the good life?"

Following the pull of Demeter, Goddess of Grain, Nurturer, Mother, leads to parenting with all of its joys and problems. Have you the range of characteristics to fulfill this role? And what new learning will you need if the role is thrust upon you, ready or not?

Playful Persephone is too often turned away under the stress of modern day living. But why not let her come romping into your life at unexpected moments? Here's a playmate. Have fun! And share her with those around you. But Persephone, Goddess Kore—"eternal girl," could keep you from growing up to be a woman. Woman or girl? Girl or woman? Why not have some of both?

Aphrodite is the Goddess of Love, Beauty and Creativity, the feminine mystique at its peak. Are you deeply sensual, sexual, passionate? Are you unconventional, reveling in raising eyebrows? Does life seem to be made for art, music, poetry, the dance? Some Aphrodites make a living at it. But Aphrodite could become a detraction from making a living, sustaining a marriage, or even maintaining good health. Yet without Aphrodite's enthusiasm and creative spark, wouldn't life be dull, indeed! If you're given a beautiful bottle of wine, you don't have to drink it all—right then, do you? No. You savor it lovingly, at the right time and with the right people. Even so with Aphrodite. Invite her in to enrich, to add sparkle, to any lifestyle you choose!

Whether you're a sea captain navigating a ship at sea, or simply trying to get from here to there by a road map, you often have to take a bearing, "where am I now?" in order to plot the next leg of your journey. So it is in your lifetrip. It's good to stop now and then and think, "Where am I in this lifetime journey of mine?

Traditional Woman? New Woman?
~ somewhere in between?

I feel I am more of a (check along the line):

"Traditional"   *"New"*
Woman   Woman

|_____|__|__|__|__|__|__|__|__|__|__|__|__|__|__|__|__|__|_____|

( ) I feel good about where I am now
( ) I'd like to move more toward
                    ( ) "Traditional" Woman
                    ( ) "New" Woman

So what *is* a "traditional" woman? How does she look and act and feel? What is it she wants most? And what about "new woman?" There are probably as many definitions of each as there are women. But there seems to be some deep fundamental difference between the two. And in you there is probably some of each, depending on the particular "mix" of your own Goddesses—the way they are now, or in a new combination you'd like to experiment with.

Whatever your Goddess mix, it's OK. And whichever way you may want to move—or not move at all, it's OK. And no matter what, you can, as the famous English poet John Ruskin so beautifully put it:

> *Make yourselves nests of pleasant thoughts. None of us know what fairy palaces we may build of beautiful thought —proof against all adversity. Bright fancies, satisfied memories, noble histories, faithful sayings, treasure houses of precious and restful thoughts, which care cannot disturb or pain make gloomy, nor poverty take away from us—houses built without hands, for our souls to live in.*

◐ Goddess Game Three

Can you punctuate this sentence in 5 different ways? Take your pencil (or pen) in hand. *Have fun!*

Woman without her man is a savage

Woman without her man is a savage

Woman without her man is a savage

Woman without her man is a savage

Woman without her man is a savage

---

5. The Goddesses: Real Or Myth?

Gods and goddesses are the products of mythology. Mythology, knowledge of myths, is a product of the minds of human beings living in ancient times. Gods and goddesses with different names came into being in the minds of men and women in various cultures around the world.

Even before written history, some say as far back as 30,000 years ago, people were making up answers to such questions as: Who made the world? Who made me? What is this "something" outside of me, bigger and more powerful than I, who seems to control my good fortune or poor fortune when I go hunting or gathering food? Who makes things grow so that I may eat, and often takes them away so I go hungry? Where will I go when I die? Since these are human questions, humans had to devise answers. So began the concept of all the powerful beings in human, animal or other form that could embody the energy humans felt controlling their fates. So gods and goddesses were born, male and female. To know them is to know yourself.

As Dr. Jean Shinoda Bolen, mentioned earlier, worked with women in her San Francisco psychiatric practice, she began to see their problems and behavior patterns falling into certain categories, often uniquely different from those set forth in conventional psychiatric literature. Reflecting on her college studies of Greek mythology and its many gods and goddesses, she undertook an in-depth study of the goddesses. She hoped to learn more of the underlying characteristics that might influence the behavior of women in each category. Her work resulted in identifying seven major goddesses.

Each goddess is an archetype—a "first form," a model, an original, embodying a unique set of behavior patterns. By helping women see her basic characteristics as an expression of a particular goddess archetype, or unique combination of them, Dr. Bolen has been able to help these women to gain a more satisfying life. In my opinion, and in those of a growing audience of her readers, her book, *Goddesses in Everywoman* does, indeed, live up to its subtitle, "A New Psychology of Woman." The goddesses set forth by Dr. Bolen have been elaborated by my own study of their mythology in the book you are now reading. The goddess concept is important to you whether you are a woman seeking deeper understanding of yourself and other women, or to a man seeking to understand you and women in general—and himself.

The unique contribution of *this* book is to bring you, through the art of photography combined with words (linguagraphics), a *feeling* for each goddess and her unique characteristics that goes beyond only words. Here is a "you-are-there" experience to bring up feelings within yourself by which you can test at "gut level" how you really do feel as you interact with the various scenarios.

Beginning with the next chapter, you will get to know your Seven Goddesses as both mythological characters and as real-life women. Then, as you move through the book, you will be able to "feel with" each one, brought down to date, as you explore options, try on roles, and learn how to use your unique goddess characteristics.

Thinking back to the "Goddess Characteristics Chart" you checked off earlier in the book, your increasing knowledge of each goddess will begin to shape your own personal goddess profile. Here, then, is your own *constellation* of goddesses. In it, some will shine brightly; others with less brilliance. And you can begin to choose options and roles to take advantage of your brightest stars and to enhance, if you wish, the lesser ones in your goddess constellation.

Whether or not you may be familiar with Shirley MacLaine's 1983 book and 1987 TV mini-series, *Out on a Limb,* a glimpse of this woman's journey toward expanding her range of goddess potentials is both heartwarming and instructive. In the television series we see a talented actress of stage and screen (played by herself) living out her strongest goddess, the brightest star in her constellation, Aphrodite and her major satellite, Persephone, only to find that "enough is not enough." Then, by paying attention to a series of seemingly casual events, she finds awakening within herself the Goddess Hestia, whose characteristics add new, exciting and deeply satisfying dimensions to her life. We also see how Shirley learns to live with and resolve conflicts between her Aphrodite-Persephone self and her Hestia values. We see, too, how she uses the characteristics of her other goddesses in timely fashion.

As we move through the next several pages looking more in depth at each of the Seven Goddesses, we will sprinkle in vignettes of the experiences of other women of our time, and times past, and their experiences in relating to their own unique patterns of the Seven Goddesses within them.

The stage is set for a new Eve and a new Adam. There is no turning back. So buckle up, and read on!

Know Your Seven Goddesses

6. Artemis

ARTEMIS, Goddess of Nature; Competitor, Sister

Zeus, the supreme deity of Greek mythology, was the father of Artemis. When Zeus asked his vivacious daughter, Artemis, what she wanted, she wished not for dolls and beautiful clothes, but for a bow, arrows and a pack of hounds. She also wanted a short tunic to let her run freely, a mountain wilderness as her special place and to have eternal chastity. She also wished for a band of woodland nymphs to follow her. Her wishes granted, she became ruggedly individualistic, highly assertive; a one-in-herself superwoman. The Romans knew her as Diana.

In the ancient myths, Artemis rushed to protect those who sought her aid. She was also quick to punish those who offended her. When Leto, her mother, was on her way to Delphi, the giant Tityus tried to rape her. Artemis, sensing her mother's peril, came quickly, took deadly aim with her bow and arrow, killing him instantly. To those who offended her, Artemis was ruthless. The hunter Actaeon accidentally came on Artemis and her nymphs bathing in a secluded pool and stood gawking at the sight. Enraged, Artemis splashed water in his face, changing him into a stag, whereupon his own hunting dogs turned on him and tore him to bits.

Love and sexuality were farthest from her mind. Nevertheless, Artemis came to love Orion. But, taking

ARTEMIS

Goddess of Nature
Competitor, Sister

advantage of her competitive spirit, jealous Apollo tricked Artemis into aiming her deadly arrow at a small dark speck in the ocean. Too late, she learned that the black speck was the head of Orion, swimming far out to sea. The one she loved had become the victim of her competitive nature.

Artemis personifies today's "feminist." She was the driving spirit behind Betty Friedan's *The Feminine Mystique,* appearing in 1963. It powered the publication of Gloria Steinem's Ms. magazine in 1972. Eleanor Smeal's early '70's work in the women's movement and presidency of NOW, the National Organization for Women, 1975-77 elicited the Artemis response in millions of women to a greater or lesser degree, to mention only three of the powerful sisterhood which has helped women recognize their Artemis qualities, learning to become the tough-minded "armored Amazon."

But this same quality of "maleness," of "hardness," has often dulled the strongly Artemis-type woman's capacity for personal intimacy; has kept men at arm's length. And after a series of attempted relationships, she may experience a feeling of such worthlessness in the interval between men that she may ultimately "give up on men." She may also have alienated women whose goddess characteristics are different from her own, tending more to what is traditionally thought to express the "feminine."

The "bible" of the Artemis sisterhood is *Ms.* magazine. Here one finds no advertising whatsoever. While the vast majority of women turn to such magazines as New Woman, Cosmopolitan, Ladies Home Journal, McCalls, Woman's Day, etc. for articles of interest, they also consume pages and pages advertising beauty aids to make them attractive to men.

It is a tribute, indeed, that a magazine can exist on the subscriptions of a loyal readership while, at the same time, seeming to eschew dealing with certain goddess characteristics important to so many women, Yet Ms. acknowledges the sexuality of some of the sisterhood in articles dealing with contraception and abortion. After all, Artemis fell in love with Orion. On the other hand, the "Health Note" section of the January/February 1995 issue features Lisa Saffron's book, *Challenging Conceptions* (Cassell; $14.95) as a "thorough, useful guide to self-insemination for women who seek to create families independently of a social father."

At the supermarket, Artemis looks for healthy, substantial foods of good value, shunning the gourmet counter. Invited to a candlelight dinner (if she accepts) she may be thinking how much nicer it would be if the tiny flame were a roaring campfire in the middle of the wilderness, and preferably without men. At the cocktail party, Artemis drinks conservatively and will most likely be found in a knot of female figures, well out of range of the male element. Contact with men will be mainly to show her independence and strength. Some men will relish such an encounter, but most will retire from the field of impending battle.

Marriage and settling down hold little attraction for the Artemis woman. While she may explore heterosexual experiences as a new adventure, sisterly feelings may dictate more lesbian leanings, attraction to a softer, more "feminine" woman than herself. In any event, she avoids being dominated in a relationship.

The ultimate Artemis of all time has been played out by Katharina in Shakespeare's play, *Taming of the Shrew*. Despite of (because of?) coming from a "good family", her coarse, tomboy ways drove suitors away, to the despair of her father who was forced to finally pay one, Petruchio, much gold to take her away. The Artemis stereotype has had a twentieth century awakening in the Broadway play, *Kiss Me, Kate.* Did Shakespeare plant the seed of the women's movement?

A strong Artemis woman gave women's liberation its first political clout. In 1848, Elizabeth Cady Stanton organized the historic Seneca Falls (N.Y.) Convention. Here some three hundred women, including Susan B. Anthony, gathered to begin the fight for women's right to vote, hold property, divorce, and be represented in the halls of legislation. Since then, scores of women activists have advanced the status of women to achieve these things and more.

But the pendulum swings. In her 1994 book, *Who Stole Feminism?,* Philosophy professor Christina Sommers has exposed a disturbing development of how a group of Artemis zealots, claiming to speak for all women, are "promoting a dangerous new agenda that threatens our most cherished ideals and sets women against men in all spheres of life." In her book, she cites case after case showing how "women have betrayed women." She especially calls attention to female professors in the echelons of higher learning who are literally training cadres of cadets to march out into the world to preach a breed of feminism that is "at odds with the real aspirations of most American women and undermines the cause of true equality." The pendulum has struck "backlash."

But a whole new world opened up for women as they were welcomed(?) into the most exclusive men's club on earth: sailing for the America's Cup. Of the twenty-eight women finally selected from hundreds of applicants, all personify Artemis.

Their occupations included an aerospace engineer, a world-class weight lifter and a professional body builder. Their sponsor, petrochemical millionaire Bill Koch, said of his team, "This race is about teamwork, tactics and a fast boat. The women have all three."

These ground-breaking, seafaring Artemis women didn't win the race, but they won the total admiration of their fellow yachts-people for a brilliant performance. They also proved that there can be a viable, valuable and enjoyable partnership between women and men.

7. Athena

ATHENA, Goddess of Wisdom

While Artemis probes her way with a point too sharp for many, so often flying in the face of what has come to be regarded as "femininity," Athena brings to the workplace, as well as the home, a feminine touch to smooth ruffled feathers, build relationships and oil the corporate machinery, whether it is an industrial giant or a "mom-and-pop" shop.

Mythology tells us that the very birth of Athena assured her appreciation for patriarchy, and a partnership with men. She never knew her mother, Metis. That goddess was the first royal consort of Zeus. When Metis was pregnant with Athena, Zeus forced her to shrink into a size so small that he swallowed her. Now he developed a violent headache. It became so unbearable that Zeus turned to Hephaestus, god of the forge, who struck him in the head with an axe. Out of the cleavage emerged Athena as a full-grown woman, clad in resplendent golden armor, carrying a spear and celebrating her entrance into the majestic company of the Olympians. She was tall, calm in appearance; majestic rather than beautiful. She was known as the goddess with the grey eyes.

As her father's right-hand woman, she was entrusted with his thunderbolt and aegis. With these symbols of power, she became protector, advisor and ally of heroic men. She aided Perseus to slay the Gorgon Medusa, the female mon-

ATHENA

Goddess of Wisdom

ster with snakes for hair, whose glance turned men into stone. "Use a mirror," she advised, "and direct your sword without meeting her gaze." Forthwith, Perseus prevailed and cut off the head of the Gorgon Medusa. Athena also helped Jason who, along with the Argonauts, built and sailed their ship to capture the golden Fleece. On another occasion, she enabled Bellerophon to tame the winged horse, Pegasus. In carrying out his twelve arduous tasks, Hercules had the advice and help of this Goddess of Wisdom.

Walking alone one evening in the shadows of the Parthenon atop The Acropolis, overlooking Athens, often referred to as "The Temple of Athena," I could almost "see"–I could certainly "feel" the presence of Athena, her grey eyes watching over her city, alert for any sign of intrusion into her world.

Among the Olympians, Athena stood with warrior generals plotting battlefield tactics. While Athena was a warrior goddess, she was not the goddess of war. She was always on the side of the victor because she did not, like Ares, the god of war, encourage rash engagements where winning would exact too great a price. Athena was a special protectress of Athens. She encouraged strife only as a means to peace.

Athena was also the goddess of crafts. She invented earthenware, spinning, weaving, the plow, rake, ox yoke, horse bridles, the chariot and even the ship. Her association with supplying this wide range of human needs was found in the many artifacts excavated from as far back as 5500 BC.

Athena is mainly a practical "let's-get-it-done" type. But she is also a woman, bringing to the workplace that essence of womankind no man can provide. What is this subtle quality? Centuries of writers have attempted to describe it. Put simply, woman is the bringer and nurturer of life. While *some* women, like *many* men see only the next quarter's bottom line of their company's profits as a guide to all their acts, a woman is much more likely to take the longer-range view. Her approach: "Yes, we could do this *now* for immediate results, but what will it do for the company's future down the line, and to the environment in which all of us must live?"

One highly placed woman executive put it this way: "You can be feminine and still be good at your job." A top male CEO: "Women tend to put in the extra effort."

In 1994, the United Nations published *Women in a Changing Global Economy: 1994 World Survey of Women in Development*. The Survey found that economic growth is closely related to the advancement of women. Where women have advanced, economic growth has usually been steady; where women have been restricted, there has been stagnation.

Claire Booth Luce (1903-1987) is cited in TIME Magazine (October 19, 1987) as *America's First Renaissance Woman*. She was a woman of great beauty, brains and energy. "Luce was," the article goes on to elaborate, "on whispering terms with history." Telling how she was friends with Winston Churchill, Chiang Kai-shek as well as American presidents from Herbert Hoover to Ronald Reagan, the article pointed out that she stormed the old boys' clubs of power without ever relinquishing her femininity.

On the job, Athena's usually tailored look will project an unself-conscious and confident look. But she will exhibit just enough femininity—the simple brooch, the smallish earrings and the latest hair-do—to attract the attention she needs from her male colleagues without exciting romantic notions.

Athena's loyalty to a Zeus-like father figure may turn her toward the lesbian life. In a same-sex relationship, she will not have to marry a man and thus be disloyal to her father. And in a same-sex life, she may feel more the equal of two partners, sharing companionship and loyalty rather than passion. Both women may be workaholics but be immune to suspicions arising from "late hours at the office." If Athena does choose a heterosexual marriage, she may tend to view it in a similar light: an arrangement to advance their mutual interests.

In her early twenties, at the height of her feminist activities, helping women to "make themselves heard," Claire Booth Luce accepted a convenient marriage to millionaire George Brokaw, 23 years her senior. She characterized him as a "bore." After six years of marriage, a handsome settlement helped her "take on the world."

Today, Athena is very much present in a number of nationally and internationally prominent figures. Hillary Rodham Clinton exemplifies the Goddess of Wisdom. Goddess Hera, The Wife, can be seen as an important star in her Goddess constellation, supporting her husband, President Bill Clinton, through many adversities. In her concern for daughter Chelsea, she demonstrates Goddess Demeter, another admirable characteristic showing how a woman can successfully listen to the guidance of more than one goddess sitting on her board of directors.

As a modern "warrior goddess," Rear Admiral Marsha Johnson Evans now heads the U.S. Navy's prestigious Naval Post Graduate School in Monterey, California. During her 32-year career in the Navy, Admiral Evans has earned many decorations and citations for exceptional service, including the Humanitarian Service Medal.

Down through history and up through time, Athena women have distinguished themselves as leaders and politically powerful. Cleopatra (Egypt, 69-30 BC) rose to heights of influence that ended in her choosing death by snake-bite. But the "Antony and Cleopatra" story will forever shine as a tribute to the Aphrodite that was her strength and her downfall.

Elizabeth I (England—1533-1603). Her great strength was her popularity. She had an instinct for adopting policies approved by her subjects.

Catherine the Great (Germany 1729-Russia 1796) completed the work begun by her husband's grandfather, Peter the Great, centralizing power and expanding territorial Russia. She also built "The Hermitage," the world's greatest art museum, covering over two acres of 3-story buildings overlooking the Neva River. I have been privileged to spend many hours amazed and fulfilled by its treasures.

Peron, Eva (Argentina—1919-1952) became a star of international politics. She was also known as the mother of the *descamisados*, the "shirtless" ones, the very poor, drawing on her Hestia and Demeter qualities.

Margaret Thatcher (England—1925-). Known as "The Iron Lady," became Europe's first woman prime minister. She was the self-proclaimed champion of the British middle class.

Benazir Bhutto (Pakistan—1953-) became the first modern woman to head a Muslim country, and the first prime minister to give birth to a child.

Indira Gandhi (India—1917-1984) generated cohesion in an incredibly diverse country with more than eight hundred million inhabitants. She is a link with the myths of her father, Nehru, and Mahatma Gandhi. Meeting her at the

Summer Palace in Bombay, I experienced Prime Minister Indira Gandhi as a woman not only of great inner strength and composure but also as a woman of delightful femininity. And the list could go on and on, and back down years of history.

The Athena woman embraces "progress." Today, technological progress may be getting out of hand. Let us hope that Athena will soften the cutting edge of "progress" by increasing her communion with her more humanistic goddesses. Athena, your power can save Gaia, Our Mother Earth, and ourselves, from "progress."

We can do
no great things–
only small things
with great love.

–Mother Teresa, b.1910
Yugoslavian Roman
Catholic missionary

8. HESTIA

HESTIA, Goddess of the Hearth and Temple
Hail, thou that are highly favored,
the lord is with thee; blessed art
thou among women

Luke—I, 28

Unlike Artemis and Athena, extroverted and active, Hestia values the life within. "Yet," to quote Jean Shinoda Bolen, "there were likenesses: On the surface, anonymous Hestia seems to have little in common with quick-to-act Artemis or with keen-minded, golden-armored Athena. Yet essential intangible qualities were shared by all three virgin goddesses, however different their spheres of interest or modes of action. Each had the one-in-herself quality that characterizes a virgin goddess. None was victimized by male deities or morals. Each had the ability to focus on what mattered to them and concentrate on that...." Influenced by Aphrodite (Goddess of Love), both Poseidon (God of the Sea) and Apollo (God of the Sun) fell madly in love with Hestia, but she refused them, swearing on oath to remain forever a virgin. Whereupon Zeus, for reasons best known to himself, bestowed upon her the honor of presiding over all sacrifices and offerings. Her place was in the very center of the temple. He also extended her influence by causing her to be worshiped in every household and in the temples of all the gods. The essence of Hestia is fire burning in a hearth. And so it

HESTIA

Goddess of Hearth and Temple

came to be, that in all temples, the hearth, a circle of stones, became central to the spirit dwelling within. And whenever a new household, or a new colony was formed, coals from the sacred fire were taken from the temple hearth to establish the fire of Hestia in the new place. Hestia finds sanctuary and contentment in a home. Going about her daily house-keeping tasks gives Hestia a sense of inner harmony. Instead of rushing to get through or feeling sorry for herself for having to do all the little things it takes to keep a house going, she moves through the work almost in a state of meditation. She is fulfilled in making a house a home.

The Hestia woman falls easily into the (old fashioned?) idea of "the good wife." Men who like a quiet, unassertive, self-sufficient woman who will acknowledge him head of the house and breadwinner will be attracted to Hestia. In his book, *Care Of the Soul,* Thomas Moore sees caring for the soul as a way to uncover "the sacredness that arises from things like cooking, music and the family."

Having sex can be satisfying for Hestia, but mainly to give her husband a good experience. Men who want a sexy woman look elsewhere. If she has lesbian leanings, it is more likely to be based on friendship than on sexuality. Today, Hestia is beginning to embrace the concept of *Sacred Pleasure,* a picture of partnership sexuality so beautifully painted by Riane Eisler in her book by that title (HarperSan Francisco, 1995). The book looks at "the key importance of sex in all human relations," and shows how more and more women and men are re-mything the sacred...relearning love...and recreating our lives and the future of sex, love and pleasure."

At work Hestia is found in traditionally feminine jobs

typing, filing and often adding a woman's caring touch by serving coffee. She stays out of office politics and gossip. In the professions, she may be the patient, sympathetic photographer. m e excellent teacher of younger children calls on Hestia's qualities. So does the nurse.

In her writings, St. Teresa of Avila reveals strong Hestia qualities. So does the well-known, present-day poet, May Sarton. Mother Teresa earned the Nobel Peace Prize for her work in bringing spiritual and physical comfort to thousands of unfortunates in India.

Clara Barton (1821-1912), founder of The American Red Cross, was Hestia in action. At the outbreak of the Civil War, calling on her Athena organizing abilities, she acted on her own initiative to obtain and distribute supplies for the relief of wounded soldiers. Not only that, but at times she exposed herself to battlefield crossfire in giving direct aid to the wounded, truly an "angel of the battlefield." In 1869, she again plunged into the task of aiding victims of the Franco-Prussian War flaming across Europe, associating herself with the International Red Cross. Returning to the United States in 1873, she established a United States branch of the Red Cross and became the first president of the American Red Cross and extended its efforts beyond war to relief in times of such other calamities as famine, flood, earthquake and other disasters.

Another Hestia powered by Athena and also, in no small way, by Artemis, love of animals, is Caroline Hebard. At 49, a housewife and mother, she became head of one of the nation's top volunteer rescue teams—with her canine partner, a handsome, super-intelligent German shepherd. Having raised four children (now 15 to 23) she made herself ready, at a moment's notice to embark on a search-and-rescue effort anywhere in the world. How did it all happen? "I began (it) to get away from kids and diapers," she told Hank Williams, her interviewer for *Parade Magazine,* September 12, 1993. "It had to do with loving the outdoors and working with dogs. It was therapy, at first, but it's become a great deal more. I've been in some pretty hairy situations," she says, but "most of all, I've learned to appreciate life."

Dedicating her book, *The Spirit of Findhorn,* Eileen Caddy wrote, "I was shown the dawn of a glorious new day, and was completely uplifted by the wonder and beauty of it." This remarkable Hestia woman was truly selected to literally sit in the center of the temple and to spread her influence around the world.

The Findhorn Community in northern Scotland came into being in 1962 "because Peter and Eileen Caddy and their colleague, Dorothy MacLean, not only had faith, but sought to act on it in their everyday lives and to demonstrate its reality and power for all people."

"Living by that faith," continues the book's Preface, "they found themselves guided to the small fishing village of Findhorn. There with their three children they lived in a caravan (mobile home), learning to attune themselves even closer to the God within and to live in harmony with the spiritual laws and truths revealed to them."

Daily Eileen listened to the voices and saw the visions given to her. Soon, on barren sand dunes were growing vegetables of size and in such profusion as to dumbfound their once suspicious village neighbors. The very spirit of Findhorn manifested for all to see and believe in the magic of what can happen when humanity is willing to work with nature, even under the most unlikely conditions.

On personal visits to the Findhorn Community over the years I have seen it grow from a few parked caravans to buildings ranging from modest homes and productive gardens and crafts shops to the Findhorn University building, a 100-foot-across pentagonal structure. In fact, I personally helped carry stones up from the beach that formed the fortress-like walls and roof. I was also guest lecturer at its formal opening. My presentation to an audience of over 400: "The Age of Findhorn."

In my treasured private talks with both Eileen and Peter Caddy, it was easy to understand how their practical spirituality materialized into the living, breathing Findhorn Community literally "from scratch." Among the very first "intentional communities," Findhorn, like the others, came into being because a tiny nucleus of people *intended* to start and live a new way of life--far from the maddening crowds and artificial "needs" of so-called civilization. On the other side of the world, in India, Acrosanti was also created as a "new age community" unbeknownst to Findhorn. There are now Findhorn satellite groups all over the United States. The "Magic of Findhorn," created in the hearthfires of Hestia may yet spread around the world.

Hestia is not a joiner or social climber. People attachment, possessions, power—all are of little importance to the Hestia woman. And one cannot help but wonder if the world would not be a better place if there were more of Hestia's characteristics among us, both of women and men.

Plain women know more about men than beautiful ones do.   –Katharine Hepburn. b. 1909
American Actress

9. Hera

HERA, Goddess of Marriage

If, as and when Artemis or Athena marry, they will be highly selective and will relate only to a man who treats them at least as equal partners in the matrimonial adventure. Hestia will make sure the man appreciates her homemaking and spiritual qualities. All three of these goddesses tend to be highly individualistic, stand on their own two feet; not needing a man to complete their lives, although they may bring valuable characteristics to a marriage. But Hera will marry just to be married. Hera, like Demeter, Persephone and Aphrodite, soon to be introduced, needs a man to round out their self-concept. Fortunately, there are many other— and very good—reasons why a woman may wish to marry.

Hera was the consort of Zeus, the god of gods of the Olympians, ruling over heaven and earth. She was the greatest of all the Olympian goddesses. The tall, stately Hera was revered and worshiped as the powerful Goddess of Marriage. The honeymoon of Zeus and Hera lasted three hundred years. During the marriage, four children were born: Hephaesas, Ares, Elithyia and Hebe. Marked with constant contention, the marriage was not a model of domestic tranquillity. Stories of constant conflict abound.

According to an account appearing in the *New Larousse Encyclopedia of Mythology* (Prometheus Press, 1968), there is

HERA

Goddess of Marriage

a story that :

> ...Hera and Zeus were arguing one day as to whether the man or the woman derived greater pleasure from the sexual act. Zeus said that women enjoyed it more, but Hera maintained that men were actually the luckier sex in this regard. The two deities decided to consult Tiresias, who had experienced the sexual act both as a man and as a woman. Tiresias sided with Zeus, saying that if the pleasures of love were divided into ten parts, the man felt only one of those parts, while the woman felt the other nine. Hera was so annoyed at being contradicted in this way that she deprived Tiresias of sight.

In another story,

> Hera participated in the beauty contest in which she was pitted against Aphrodite and Athena, with Paris acting as judge at the request of the three goddesses. Hera lost, Aphrodite won. The anger of Hera carried considerable weight, and in the Trojan War she sided against the Trojans in revenge for Paris' refusal to award her the prize.

As their marriage wore on, Zeus resumed his former promiscuous ways, evoking Hera's raging jealousy. Here it's interesting to note that the Hera woman is most likely to direct her anger not at her husband, but at "the other woman" or her children. At one point, Zeus tried to conceal his children to protect them from Hera's violent, vindictive anger by hiding them underground.

Hera had children more as "the thing to do" rather than desiring them to enjoy motherhood. Her son, Hephaestus,

God of the Forge, was born with a club foot. Disappointed, she threw him out of the company of the Olympians. In the case of her other son, Ares, perhaps her own combative tactics subconsciously taught him the qualities that made him the God of War!

The Hera woman values the "r" in "Mrs." She cannot understand the woman who is proud to be "Ms." While she may get some satisfaction with an on-going relationship, she yearns for the commitment of marriage. With a man she is *somebody*. Without one, she is a nobody. And the higher the status of the man, the more "somebody" she will be. Nancy Reagan is said to be an archetype of the strongly Hera wife when she said "Ronnie is my reason for being happy."

Wallis Warfield had no compunction about turning on so powerful an Hera image that a King gave up his throne. Twice married before, she wed the Prince of Wales who would become King Edward III. British royalty could not marry a divorcée. Rather than lose the love of Wallis, the King abdicated the throne of the King of England. Hera triumphed. She not only married to become *somebody* but also, according to all accounts, found love.

Rose Kennedy, mother of President Jack Kennedy and an exemplary Hera as wife of Joseph Kennedy, found herself in the same situation as Goddess Hera married to Zeus. But she didn't let it keep their marriage from working, as well as producing nine children. Joe Kennedy took as his mistress screen star Gloria Swanson. "If she resented me," wrote Gloria in her memoirs, "she never gave any indication of it." Swanson wondered if Rose was "a fool, a saint, or a better actress than she was" recounts historian Doris Kearns Goodwin in her 1984 best-selling biography, *The Fitzgeralds and the Kennedys.* Rose Kennedy: Intelligent Hestia triumphant.

Until quite recently, our culture considered that woman's main accomplishment was "getting married." The big church wedding was the symbol of Hera's fondest dream. Today, the goals of more education, a career and simply "being out there where the action is" are challenging Hera's fundamental values, but the Goddess Hera still holds sway in the hearts and minds of many women. Too often, however, trying to "have it all," the Hera archetype and her husband are hard put to continue the commitment she so deeply desires.

Perhaps at such a point, Hera should try turning things around as suggested by Dr. Gina Ogden. A marriage and family counselor in Cambridge, Massachusetts, she writes in *Ladies Home Journal, August, 1995,* "Want to make love like you used to?" "The secret," she continues is putting your overcommitted life on hold, and letting yourself go, really go....It's allowing yourself to say, 'The hell with the laundry and the bills today. I'm going to put those things on hold and have some *fun* for a change.' " She advises visualizing reruns of exciting times. One of her clients reported how it worked for her and her husband. One night, after viewing a torrid love scene in a movie, they left the theater and had "urgent sex" in the back seat of their minivan. "I replay that scene at least three times a day while I'm at work," she said, "so by the time I get home I can't wait to get my hands on him." A lot of Aphrodite here!

Because of the usual wear and tear of a marriage relationship, and the ever watchful eye of Hera to detect any tendencies toward unfaithfulness in her husband, the man may tire of the walls she seems to build around him and increasingly seek escape, turning his attentions elsewhere. It is true that some Hera women, once having achieved marriage, become less interested in sex; the glue that held their early relationship together may have come unstuck.

In such a situation, Hera will naturally begin to suffer. "Loving" her man may become more of a duty. And even though it begins to appear that they are simply not suited to each other, Hera would rather continue the mental and often physical pain of "staying in there" rather than let go. Divorce is unthinkable. She begins to measure her degree of "love" by the depth of her suffering: A woman who loves too much. When such a woman reaches out to other goddess characteristics for help, she will find strength and a sense of one-in-herself in Artemis and Athena. Her husband may react by a new admiration for her; there may be a new beginning for both. Or, the relationship may end, leaving her stronger and wiser for having called on the other goddesses within.

Down through the ages, the intelligent Hera woman has been able to help her husband appreciate all the womanness she can give him.

10. Demeter

DEMETER, Goddess of Grain, Nurturer, Mother

For Artemis, children were somebody else's business. For Athena, they might go with the territory. Hestia would warm and cozy children. Hera would have them because "it was the thing to do," and children would help her keep her man. But Demeter wants to *have* them—give birth, feed them, mother them.

In Greek mythology Demeter was worshiped, in the words of Homer, as "that awesome goddess with her beautiful hair...," presiding over bountiful harvests, literally nurturing and mothering the Universe. Even her name contains the Greek word for mother: *meter. De* is the delta, or triangle, a female genital sign known as "the letter of the vulva" in the Greek sacred alphabet. In India, it was the Yoni Yantra, or yantra of the vulva. The Romans called her Ceres, hence our word "cereal," primal nourishment.

Demeter's mothering is most famous for having produced her daughter Kore with her husband Zeus. Demeter tried always to keep Kore at her side, watching over as a mother goose with her treasured only duckling. The name Kore meant "Maiden," and she was destined never to quite grow up.

Kore was a beautiful, carefree child and was sometimes allowed to wander in the fields of Nysa. As she grew into an

DEMETER

Goddess of Grain, Nurturer, Mother

alluring young woman, she still roamed the fields soaking up the beauty of Nature. One day, as she was gathering flowers with her companions, she suddenly noticed a narcissus of such beauty she ran to pick it up. Then, just as she bent over to grasp its stem, the earth opened up and Hades appeared. Seizing her, he dragged her into his black chariot and dove down into the depths of the earth. Zeus had already promised Hades to have Kore as his wife. Now, Kore, the maiden, no longer the carefree girl, came to learn the dark mysteries. Hades made her "Queen of the Underworld" and gave her the name Persephone.

As her daughter disappeared into the earth, Demeter heard her desperate cry for help. But she arrived too late. Kore was gone. "Then," says the poet of the Homeric hymn, "bitter sorrow seized her heart....Over her shoulder she threw a somber veil and flew like a bird over land and sea, seeking here, seeking there...." For nine days, using her Goddess Power, Demeter ranged the world, "bearing flaming torches in her hands." Finally, consulting the divine Hellos, she learned that Zeus himself had awarded her beloved daughter to his brother, Hades, to wife.

In a rage of despair, Demeter withdrew from Olympus and sought refuge in the cities, disguised as a wrinkled old woman. Needing so desperately to "mother," she took employment as a nursemaid, bringing up her charge, Demophoon, "as a god." One day she revealed her true self and commanded a temple to be built for her. Here she sat, brooding over the loss of her daughter. Her wrath was so great, she commanded that nothing could be born, nothing could grow even if it destroyed the human race, until her daughter was returned to her. Finally Zeus was forced to effect Kore's rescue. Mother and daughter were reunited.

But now there was a problem: Hades had given Persephone pomegranate seeds to eat. This fruit was a symbol of marriage and the effect of eating it was to make the union of man and wife indissoluble. Then, keeping his promise, Hades returned her up through the earth into her mother's waiting arms. "Surely you have not eaten there in the depth and you can come to live with me in Olympus. But if you have, then you must return back into the depths of the earth." Then Kore admitted she had eaten of the pomegranate. Demeter was to lose her daughter again! Desperately she appealed to Zeus. In compromise, Zeus commanded that Persephone should live with her husband for one-third of the year, spending the other two-thirds with her mother. Demeter agreed and soon the earth blossomed forth providing beauty and nourishment for all.

When Demeter is the major goddess influencing today's woman, her whole desire is to become pregnant, have a baby and nurture its growth. And the more babies, the better. The Demeter woman is more likely to marry early, forgoing further education for the joy of having babies and raising a family. If she becomes "accidentally" pregnant, she will agonize over an abortion, although it may be clearly in the best interests of all. The Artemis, Athena or Hera woman could easily decide to have an abortion.

While being a biological mother is the Demeter woman's most powerful drive, the nurturing instinct develops strongly. The most generous of all the goddesses of Greek mythology, Demeter's archetype today showers her affection on all around her. Her children feel her concern, sometimes too much. Here, wanting to "do things" for them and demanding their responses of appreciation can begin to come on as restrictive. Her "super-mothering" can begin to squelch instead of nurture. In familiar words, she keeps them "tied to her apron strings."

Cast in the role of Hera triumphant in the previous chapter, Rose Kennedy was also a redoubtable Demeter. "At 104," recounts *People Weekly* magazine (February 6, 1995) "Rose Fitzgerald Kennedy, the steel-willed founder of a political dynasty, dies the way she lived—surrounded by her remarkable family."

Not only did Rose Kennedy produce nine children, but she took time to discipline and inspire them. "Mother would have made a great featherweight," Ted Kennedy once said. "She had a mean right hand." During the eulogy for his mother, Edward Kennedy recalled, "Mother always thought her children should strive for the highest place." The matriarch saw three of her children elected to the U.S. Senate and one of them rise to the Presidency.

The Goddess Power of Rose Kennedy came from her successful combination of Hera, Demeter, and very often calling upon her Athena. Nor did she neglect the Goddess of Love and Beauty, Aphrodite, to charm her way toward her goals.

Some women adopt whole families of children to distribute their mothering talents among many. After her break-up with Woody Allen, Mia Farrow set about adopting more than a dozen children. But too often a woman cannot, or will not, find a way to extend her powerful mothering needs outside their immediate family. The resulting concentration—even to adding the final touch to her daughter's cooking, can result in "non-mothering," in keeping offspring from learning to stand on their own two feet.

Fearing the loss of her children, the Demeter woman may begin having "empty nest" feelings even before her children depart into their own worlds, bringing on depression. The depressed Demeter, formerly the very soul of bountiful giving, may now begin to withhold, even as Goddess Demeter, depressed by her daughter's absence, stopped all things growing, threatening famine to all the earth. Nor is her husband untouched by her depression. While a man enjoys a sense of being cared for, over-mothering can also turn a man off, making him feel restricted instead of being loved.

To counteract the super-mothering urge, the predominantly Demeter woman can begin to "mother" herself. She can call on Goddess Athena and organize her days to make time for doing things *she* would enjoy: gardening, crafts, painting, music, etc. Reaching out to Goddess Aphrodite, she can lighten up a bit and add sparkle to her life and to those around her. She can begin to experience satisfaction in the fun of give and take, instead of drearily plodding along on the one-way street of all giving.

Sex is secondary for the Demeter woman. Sex is a way of having babies and providing a nurturing environment for her mothering needs. The sensuality of breast feeding her baby may be more important than sex with her husband. Often, to her husband's dismay, she'd just as soon cuddle as consummate the act. Again, getting in touch with Aphrodite could do much to enhance marriage and foster the feelings of fatherhood in her man as they both share in the body/mind/spirit creativity of another human life.

Will today's growing biotechnology eliminate motherhood, as it is already doing away with so many of our human attributes? "Algeny," says Jeremy Rifkin, "will radically transform our conception of life. It will sweep Darwinism aside and be used to legitimize the coming biological revolution. It will utterly change the world our children inherit." In his book, *Algeny,* in collaboration with Nicanar Perlos (The Viking Press, 1983), Rifkin sets forth the proposition that "our decision to develop biotechnology is potentially far more dangerous than our decision to split the atom. Beyond the promise of miracles may lie the reality of extinction." Rifkin concludes: "Now that we have it within our power to refashion all of nature in order to secure our future, we need to ponder whether such is our right."

It will require the power and wisdom, not only of Demeter, but of all seven of our goddesses to enable the human dimension to flower instead of being "cybernated" into oblivion.

11. Persephone

PERSEPHONE, Goddess Kore, Eternal Maiden

The Goddesses Artemis, Athena, Hestia, Hera and Demeter all had quite distinguishable characteristics and personality patterns. Persephone, on the other hand, as Kore, the Greek name for "maiden" was somewhat of a chameleon. She was, as the Romans later called her personification, "aeterna puella," eternally a girl.

Persephone never wanted to grow up. Due to Demeter's "super-mothering" she was not allowed to and yet, when she did, it happened very fast. One remembers from the preceding introduction to Goddess Demeter, how Persephone was kidnapped and taken to the Underworld by Hades. There she learned to deal with the dark side of life, an accomplishment, according to renown psychiatrist Carl Jung, all too frequently neglected in rounding out a life.

A Persephone woman may never grow out of her Kore "little girl" role. Or, she may, with advancing years and "living through the fires of Hell," an Underworld created by her own indiscretions, emerge as a wise elder, able to guide others as they move through dark periods of their lives.

The woman beset by Persephone qualities has a hard time deciding, "what I want to be when I grow up." In fact, she is afraid of growing up. If she does, she will lose her freedom. She will have to make decisions, take responsibility.

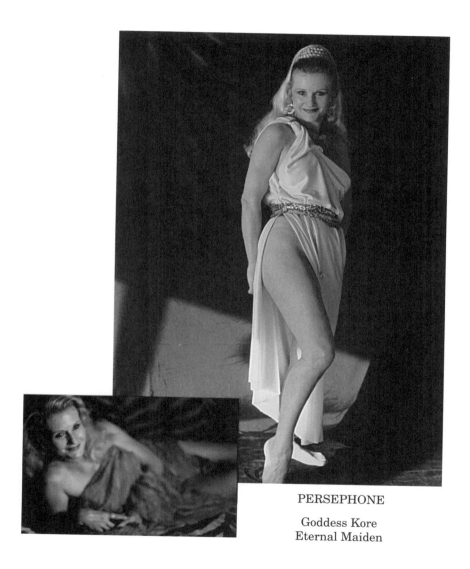

PERSEPHONE

Goddess Kore
Eternal Maiden

She often seems to be a spectator on her own life. Relationship, marriage or career seem "not for real," something to be played at. And this sense of unreality makes her feel powerless. Feeling lack of power, she turns manipulative. "I'll get him (or her) to do it if I have to make up a few lies and even cheat a little." She will do this as a way of "getting by" instead of facing a situation head on and choosing the best solution.

Marilyn Monroe (1926-1962) was born Norma Jean Mortenson. As a troubled child, seductress, desperate actress and sex symbol she led a tempestuous life. During her brief, almost bizarre career, she moved, at times, among nationally prominent figures and on the fringes of politics in her dalliance with both John and Robert Kennedy. Her drug-troubled life ended mysteriously.

The actress was Persephone personified. Father unknown and deserted by her unstable mother to live in a succession of foster homes, she was married at 16. Photos of her modeling at five dollars an hour quickly attracted a model agency to farm her out as a "clothes horse." Emphasizing her thirty-six inch bust she became a pin-up and magazine cover girl. In a contract with 20th Century Fox, she was renamed Marilyn Monroe. Unpromising at first—only bit parts—she finally danced and sang in *Ladies of the Chorus* for Columbia. Back with Fox, her role in *The Asphalt Jungle* paid her $500 a week instead of the original $125. *Gentlemen Prefer Blondes* assured her stardom and put her hand and footprints in fresh cement on Hollywood Boulevard.

Now the limelight took its toll and Marilyn began arriving late at the set and developing a dependency on drugs. Her marriage to star baseball player Joe DiMaggio lasted nine months. Nearly thirty, she briefly married playwright Arthur Miller. During filming of his *Misfits*, an overdose of drugs committed her to a psychiatric hospital.. Photographer of the rich and famous Henri Cartier-Bresson called her the "incarnation of the myth that in France we call "l'éternal féminin."

Marilyn Monroe will continue to intrigue us. In 1995, her place in the history of woman was assured when the United States Post Office produced a postage stamp featuring her trademark eye-catching feminine proportions. The first issue was sold out in three days. Viva la Marilyn!

While Marilyn Monroe's "Persephone" ended tragically, it doesn't have to be that way for the vast majority of predominately Persephone women. Instead, they can add a sense of playfulness in a world surely in need of "lightening up." Nor will it require a troubled childhood such as Marilyn's to be able to contribute to the world's happiness.

Today, Persephone woman tends to take on the qualities expected of her by whomever she might be with. Her compliant nature makes her seek her identity in others. Her over-zealous, often charming efforts to please are a way of escaping responsibility. As mother's little girl, she has become accustomed to leaving decisions up to her parent. A father may also create and reinforce a Persephone offspring by demanding a strict regimen of behavior "to protect her from consequences" or simply, as she grows toward womanhood, because of subconscious jealousy.

As the carefree, flower-picking child-woman before her abduction by Hades, Persephone was not aware of her sexual attractiveness. But given her compliant nature and living in the traditional cultures of today,, she falls easily into the role of "sex kitten." In this character, she is likely to be continually surprised at being taken advantage of by men. Often, her seeming sexuality may be disappointing as she may lack the maturity to experience the depths of passion.

Before Persephone grows through Kore and into her other role as Queen—if she does—her whole behavior pattern might well be summed up as "spoiled brat." Her Kore characteristics, however, may stem more from her upbringing than from inborn temperament. And her "world owes me a living and a good time" attitude is not confined to one gender. A "male Persephone" may develop in the same way and for the same reasons. If they ever get together they can count on MAD—Mutually Assured Destruction.

A Persephone will not likely *choose* marriage. She will be abducted into it. She sees it as a trip into captivity, even as the mythological Hades kidnapped her to be his bride and Queen of the underworld. And again, she did not return to the upper world of her own volition, but because of Demeter's wishes. And by eating the forbidden pomegranate seeds, she was allowed to remain above ground only two-thirds of the year. The other third, she was to live with Hades and his murky denizens as Queen of the Underworld.

The kidnapping of Patty Hearst is a contemporary analog of the Persephone mythology. An over-sheltered daughter is whisked away by a modern-day Hades, a "Persephone man," and forced to live underground. Ultimately, she adopts their gun-toting ways and is respected, even idolized for her show of rebellion against society. She became, indeed, the Queen of the Underworld until rescued by her Zeus-and-Demeter-like parents, a pair of down-to-date Olympians.

A Persephone woman may spend much time in front of a

mirror. Preoccupied with "How do I look," she spends enormous energy on make-up and clothes. She must please at any price. If her efforts fail to continually bolster self-esteem, she may become depressed and fade into the woodwork. Or she may impose upon herself the scourge of anorexia (not eating) or bulimia (eating and throwing up).

Of all the Seven Goddesses, Persephone, in her teenage and early twenties, is most likely to choose an eating disorder joining today's fad for becoming fashion-model thin. A Sunday feature in the *Herald*, Monterey County, July 2, 1995, headlines, "Teenage girls' worries...the pressure to be pretty, boys and sex." The article goes on to quote one high school girl as saying, "they talk about weight and feeling ugly." Another high school girl put it this way: "You see all the models on TV. There's so much pressure for girls to look like them." Another said, "If we see girls with thin stomachs, we want that stomach." "There are a lot of teens (girls) at our school don't want to eat," mourned another.

Some men, and some women, who create fashion model images are not only profiting handsomely *but destroying the lives* of increasingly thousands of young women. I personally know of one 18-year-old girl who has been "put away" for a whole year to an institution that will work on re-orienting her to "reality" and normal eating. Her parents had to re-mortgage their home to pay for it.

When will these Persephone types learn that what a man really wants in is his arms is not a gangly scarecrow skeleton but the full rich body of a "not-afraid-to-be-a-woman" woman?

With all the negatives that seem to come with being a Persephone, some women, particularly Artemis and Athena types, may find more happiness by taking on some of Persephone's softness and her compliant ways. Persephone, on the other hand, can learn the role of a more self-confident, responsible and desirable person by reaching out toward some of the characteristics of Artemis and Athena, as well as the richer inner life of Hestia. Because of her many problems, Persephone may have more ways to grow than any of the other goddesses.

When choosing
between two evils,
I always like
to try the one
I've never tried
before...

−Mae West (1892-1980)
American Actress

12. Aphrodite

APHRODITE, Goddess of Love, Beauty, Creativity

There is no better way to begin an introduction to the seventh and most unique of the elemental goddesses than in the words of Jean Shinoda Bolen herself, as she sets forth "A New Psychology of Women" in her aforementioned book, *Goddesses In Everywoman:*

> Aphrodite, Goddess of Love and Beauty, I place in a category all her own as the alchemical goddess, a fitting designation for the magic process or power of transformation that she, alone, had. In Greek mythology, Aphrodite was an awesome presence who caused mortals and deities (with the exception of the three virgin goddesses) to fall in love and conceive new life. For Pygmalion, she turned a statue into a living woman (in contrast, Athena turned people into stone). She inspired poetry and persuasive speech, and symbolizes the transformative and creative power of love.

While Aphrodite shows some of the characteristics of Artemis, Athena, Hestia, Hera, Demeter and Persephone she is in a class by herself. "Unconventional" will be the key word for the Golden Goddess, as was her birth. In Greek mythology, Cronos, father of main-line Olympian gods, took a sickle and cut off the genitals of his own father, Uranus. Then he cast them into the sea, causing a white foam to

APHRODITE

Goddess of Love, Beauty, Creativity

spread around them. As sperm and sea mixed, Aphrodite took form, emerging from her oceanic conception as a fully grown goddess. Botticelli immortalized the happening in his painting, "Birth of Venus," the name by which the Romans knew her, showing Aphrodite standing nude on a seashell, golden hair flying in the wind. She was blown ashore and escorted by Eros (Love) and Himeros (Desire) into the assembly of the Olympians to become one of them.

Aphrodite had many romantic liaisons with both gods and mortal men. With Ares, God of War, she had three children. From this union a perfect balance was struck between the two most powerful passions, love and war, to produce the lovely daughter they named Harmonia. From another union, this time with Hermes, Messenger of the Gods, was born Hermaphroditus, a bisexual god who had the beauty and sexual characteristics of both parents. Thus was born the concept of androgyny, the existence, in one person, of the characteristics traditionally considered either masculine or feminine.

Aphrodite's most famous mortal lover was Adonis, a man of great masculine beauty. The fearlessness of the young hunter caused Aphrodite concern for his life. Unheeding of her advice, Adonis wounded a wild boar which attacked, tearing him to pieces, sending him to the depths below. Later he was reunited with Aphrodite on his return from the Underworld where he had also become the lover of Persephone.

While her "chemistry" attracts both women and men, Aphrodite's main attraction is to and for men. The Aphrodite archetype is a gift to all women who love to love. The woman who has not yet fallen under the magic, transformational spell of love would do well to listen to Aphrodite as she whispers in her ear, "Try me!" Men, bathed in the golden glow of Aphrodite, feel more godlike than ordinary mortal man. For women and men alike, Aphrodite's presence charges the very air with erotic electricity; sensuality and sexuality are magnified; music, fragrances, touch and taste take on new excitement.

In the grand scheme of things, we have no difficulty acknowledging that great works of art, engineering achievement and the building of whole civilizations have come out of intertwining man-woman sexual instincts. Great paintings, music, dance, writing and other works of art owe their power and beauty to the transformative alchemy of Aphrodite. Sexual passion—and the deprivation of its fulfillment, have sharpened the senses of creativity to peaks not possible to achieve for a woman or man who denies the creative powers Aphrodite sends coursing through the blood.

The Aphrodite archetype falls in love easily and often. Judea-Christian, Muslim and other patriarchal cultures tend to picture such a woman as a temptress, adulteress or simply a whore, degrading the standards of morality. Actually, these patriarchal reactions represent masculine fear of the female's exotic power. The sexy woman is to be controlled, not loved. Instead, men fight wars. How different things might be if men adopted the slogan, "Make love, not war!"

Young women are given little help in handling Aphrodite's insistent drives. Sex education in school is still controversial and often nonexistent. Girls and boys are left to the mercy of the instincts that produce life on earth. Caring for a million pregnant teenagers and their mostly unwanted babies each year seems preferable to dealing with the power of Aphrodite. What if the young were helped to enjoy their sexuality safely and in moderation, could they not, in later years, bring the joy of co-creativity into even simple, everyday living as they create not only children, but a home modest though it may be, in which they may experience the arts of living? The peaceful cultures of the South Sea Islands have been doing this for centuries. Instead of fighting Aphrodite, they have used her power in creating a more lovable and livable world. Teenagers are encouraged to experiment with sex early as a beautiful experience, not something "naughty" or "dirty" to be done in the dark and carried as a guilt trip that may turn girls into drug addicts or boys into rapists.

Naturally, men are attracted to the golden glow of what is pictured as the typical Aphrodite woman. Yet women with less-than-good-looks who have that "Aphrodite something" never seem to lack men in their lives. Their magnetism is an easy-going sensuality and a natural, warm personality; nor are they afraid to touch or hug. But Aphrodite may attract the kind of man who may not be good for her. To keep from being used, she will need to call on Artemis, Athena or Hestia. If she goes all out for loving a man who may be a male version of Persephone, she may find herself in the book *Smart Women; Foolish Choices* (Clarkson N. Potter, Inc., 1985) by two practicing psychologists, Dr. Connell Cowan and Dr. Melvyn Kinder. They ask, "Why is it that so many successful women end up with the wrong man?" In 204 pages, they answer the question.

At first look, one may say of Dolly Parton, "Oh, there's another Persephone 'Marilyn Monroe' type." But look again at what she's done. First of all, the sexy blonde was cited as "Woman of the Year" in *Ms.* Magazine, January 1977, among the twelve selected nationwide. None other then Gloria Steinem, editor of *Ms.* and a major mover and shaker in the Women's Movement, heads her article lauding Parton: "Dolly Parton—for creating popular songs about real women, for turning feminine style into humor and power and understanding to the mountain people of Tennessee." And I would like to add, "to all men and women everywhere who have ever seen her perform on stage and screen, a sense of what Goddess Power projected by Aphrodite can be."

Steinem continues: "If feminism means each of us finding our unique power and helping other women to do the same, Dolly Parton certainly has done both." Continuing, the article shows how Dolly, a Tennessee mountain child in a poor family of 12 began playing guitar, and writing and singing her own songs at the age of seven to produce, over the years, more than sixty albums. In her "9 to 5", such lyrics as "Tumble out of bed and stumble to the kitchen; pour myself a cup of ambition..." have become anthem for millions of working women.

Dolly Parton is also a shining example of combining the Goddess Power of Hestia and Athena in her concerns and actions to help her mountain neighbors. As a successful business woman, she built Dollywood, a theme park that has brought jobs and understanding to the mountain folk and attracted over a million tourists a year. Steinem's final tribute to Parton: "She has taken all the ridiculed modern symbols of femininity, from make-up and platform shoes to wigs and false eyelashes, and infused them with humor and conscious power."

Persephone-like Marilyn Monroe was attracted like a moth to flame until the limelight of stardom singed her wings. Dolly Parton, on the other hand, used her alchemical Aphrodite power not only to reach stardom, but accomplished solid creativity to the benefit of herself and others.

Demeter wanted sex to have babies. Aphrodite has babies, if she has them, because she wants sex. But although motherhood is not her basic drive, when Aphrodite does have children, she tends to foster their creativity and share with them her joy of living. In the world of work, she can be an inspired teacher, a sympathetic counselor. Aphrodite shuns the repetitive work of office or laboratory, or housekeeping. She is likely to take a less well-paid job that involves her creativity than one with less appeal but paying more. She liberates her best self working in art, music, drama and their various supportive services where she can express her own talents and interact with other people. The Goddess Power of Aphrodite illuminates the scene for all of us.

⬤ GODDESS GAME FOUR

Who said what?

Now that you've met all the goddesses within you, it's time to get better acquainted. Here's the next step. Enjoy! (Of course, you may look back to get a refresher)

Artemis?
Athena?
Hestia?
Hera?
Demeter?
Persephone?
Aphrodite?

Write in the Goddess's name:

I like to "keep the home fires buring." I enjoy making a house into a warm and cozy home. It's my life.

1. _____

I can't understand women who simply want to bother with such petty things as "homemaking" and all those housekeeping chores when there is so much to be done in the world. We've got to change things!

2. _____

It's exciting and challenging to be out there in the world of business, working with men and women who produce things, who make things work.

3. _____

My life would be very incomplete without a man to share it with, to be my husband. I can't understand women who want to leave the "r" out of "Mrs."

4. _____

Motherhood; having children, watching them grow; nurturing them. What more could any woman want?

5. _____

Sure my voltage goes up when I see an attractive man! But I also get a terrific charge out of music, art and just being with exciting people. Life is a party!

6. _____

"Will she ever grow up?" I know that's what some people think of me. But then, they don't know that (if/and) when I do grow up, I can help them understand the dark side of themselves

7._____

Key: You may wish to compare your answers with:
   1. Hestia 2. Artemis 3. Athena 4. Hera
   5. Demeter 6. Aphrodite 7. Persephone

13. Who Is Your Leading Lady?

Throughout the remainder of the book, you will recognize many of the Goddess characteristics portrayed by the model—and in yourself. You will have more appreciation for your brightest star, your most prominent goddess, your "leading lady." You may also begin to feel conflicts between two or more of the goddesses within you. The trick is to be "chairman of the board." When faced with decisions, hear them all out, talk them out with a friend, then *you* decide which one you want to step forward, exhibit her characteristics, strengths and strategies to get you where you want to go, feeling like you want to feel.

At work, for example, you may want to call on Athena, organizer and planner. At home you may want to play the creative and unconventional Aphrodite, or perhaps a compliant Persephone, to the man in your life. Or, your work may demand creativity, enthusiasm and such social contact as an advertising agency executive, for example, while at home you re-charge your batteries in little domestic tasks, without a sense of pressure or need to please anyone but the goddess Hestia within you.

You can learn to "shift gears" among your goddesses, and smoothly. When you do, you will feel more in control of your life and enjoy each of your goddesses in turn, or on call, knowing they are there when you need them.

In addition to clarifying which goddess is the brightest

star in your own constellation and which one or ones you want to play supporting roles, you can now see that you can choose which characteristics to emphasize in which situation. "Timing is everything," someone once said. But, if not everything, there is probably a time and a place for each of your goddesses to "be themselves"—to make you feel good in a given situation. And don't worry about being consistent. Consistency may well be "the virtue of little minds," as one of my delightful old college professors used to say.

Who Am I?

Think about it. If you were the only person in the world, how would you ever find out *who* you are? There would be no one to compare yourself with. You might not even be conscious you were a human being. There you'd be, just walking around among the trees, the rocks, the rivers and the other animals. You wouldn't even have a name. You would not be a "who." You'd be a "what."

So the way we know who we are is by the way in which we relate to other people. We develop a "who"—a self, by ways in which others relate to us. The more we observe and understand this interaction between ourselves and others, the more self-understanding we acquire.

As a part of the territory through which you will pass as you read the rest of this book, you will find scenarios, games, and things to do to enliven the journey that will take you, in the words of Socrates, through the great arch of "Know Thyself," and, I would like to add, *like* yourself—better.

Sometimes I wonder who I really am

14. 2,500,000,000 Goddesses
—each one different,
and one of them is YOU!

"So I'm only one of two-and-one-half billion women who populate Planet Earth. How can I be unique, how can I be *me* in all that mob?" you ask. Well, you are already unique. You came here put together that way. There's nobody in the whole world just like you because your billions of brain cells are arranged differently from those of any other woman alive. These, and a few more billion body cells make you think and act like nobody else. Look around you. See the differences in how each person walks, talks, wears clothes, not to mention differences in faces, body build and hundreds of other ways. And all this uniqueness in spite of the fact that each has the same number of arms, legs, eyes and kinds of equipment (almost!). Even identical twins are not really alike. I knew two gorgeous, red-headed women whom I could not tell apart at a distance of ten feet—until we all got in the hot tub.

Looking back at the Goddess Characteristic Chart on page 21, you will remember that each of the seven goddesses has ten major qualities that influence the way each type thinks and acts. These, of course, are only the most prominent characteristics. Many more than ten could be listed for each. But to keep our idea manageable, let's stick with the ten. All right, we have 7 x 10 = 70. But the possibilities for using these are 70 x 70 or 4,900 combinations of goddess characteristics that could be put into action! "But," you say, "I'm really strong in only three of the Goddesses. Fair enough, so you still have 30 x 30 = 900 different

possibilities of going about a job, making love, raising a child or whatever you may want to do.

"How, " you ask, "do I go about pulling all these billions of cells together in a pattern that will get me where I want to go?" The very fact that you're reading this book means you have a good start, here and now. And no matter what, you can start where you are and move ahead as fast and as far as your learning rate and capacity will let you. And you'll never know to what levels of achievement you may go until you begin moving—in your worklife, your lovelife or any other department of living.

This "multilevel philosophy" of learning and doing, referred to earlier, has been used by over 61,000,000 people of all ages around the globe to improve their reading-thinking skills. It has happened because I started where I was forty-four years ago with thirty-two seventh grade girls and boys in a country school in Florida and moved toward building a system that would provide for the individual differences in learning rate and capacity of each student in the entire class of thirty-two and with only one teacher: me. Because each student experienced success with multilevel learning, the method took flight and spread, over a period of four decades, to the millions around the world. So start where you are. It will literally pull you ahead, level by level, to where you want to go. Your own energy and intelligence will determine how fast and how far it will take you .

Now here's a thought. When you consider taking a job, creating a product or developing a service, ask yourself: Will what I am getting into give me satisfaction as *both* an individual and as a member-of-society? Can I be *me*, and at the same time, have consideration for the rest of the five billion women and men out there, and those here around me? If you can say "Yes" to both of these, you've hit a happy option and one that can take you as fast and as far as your learning rate and capacity—and your energy, will let you, in any of the number of roles you may choose.

Man

The woman becomes pregnant,

Woman

and bears a child.

Man and woman united for procreation.

The family; man with his wife and children.

From *The Book of Signs,* "…all manner of symbols used from the earliest times to middle ages by primitive peoples and Early Christians." Collected and drawn by Rudolf Koch. Translated from the German by Vyvyan Holland. By permission of Dover Publications, Inc.

15. Turning Options Into Choices

Some say the Women's Movement has given women too confusing an array of options. Knowing your Goddess profile will help you turn a flurry of options into wise choices.

You don't need anyone to tell you that probably the biggest conflict in a woman's life is "children or career?" Now, with over sixty percent of all women in the United States working outside the home (in Russia, it's over 80%), many women are trying to have both, and with varying degrees of success and good feelings about themselves, depending on which of their Goddesses is exerting the most pull. One alleviating factor will be an increase in child care centers sponsored by industry, government and private enterprise. Another alternative is women and men switching roles, the timid arising of the "house-husband." Still another, made increasingly possible by the computer, is working in one's own home. But the vast majority of women rush off to the workplace each morning, too often torn between staying home as a full time mother and homemaker or assuming the role of "superwoman," trying to do both.

Superwoman, many are finding, is not for every woman. Many are feeling that the required extra energy and organizing abilities required are simply not there and that "something's got to give." They are beginning to ask: "Is it worth it to expend all that extra energy, endure uncertain child care and come home each night to do-it-all anyway just to have the extra income? And is this freedom or slavery on a treadmill?

Am I being caught up in the Great American Mad Rush for 'things?' If enough is enough, is more really better?"

The following scenarios may dramatize your very own emotions and help you to consider which of your Goddesses is exerting the most influence on you. As you move through the book, you will be able to answer these questions more in depth, based on your increasing understanding of each of your Seven Goddesses.

Children and/or Career?

How much of you will be fulfilled. . . . . . ?

If marriage

who owns it?   **who does it?**   **who's responsible?**

You? He? Both?   **You? He? Both?**   **You? He? Both?**

When you walk out the door, will you feel...

Like this ? . . .   or like this . . . . ?

FREEDOM

who'll do it?   —to have ideas?   a business lunch?

You? He? Both?   —to be a person   ... to be "me"

16. *"Traditional Woman"*

Just as I was becoming steeped in the "new woman" and looking for a way to represent the other half, there in the car dealer's service waiting room I struck up a conversation with an interesting looking just-past-midlife woman also awaiting her car repair. She turned out to be the wife of the municipal judge of a Central California community, 57, mother of 6 children, 21-36, five boys and one girl. I mentioned my work on the Goddess book and asked if she'd like to do a chart while waiting. She would. I explained that as part of my research, I'd rather not talk more about the chart, which would be a part of the book, until after she'd checked off her responses. After five or six minutes she handed it back. "Most interesting," I commented, glancing over it, "and thank you."

"You know," she said, "they've taken the dignity out of being a woman."

"How?" I inquired.

"They've taken the dignity out of being a wife and mother. Now women want to get out and be in the professions and do all sorts of men's work and have the privileges of men but not take the responsibilities. And if they can't succeed at it, they fall back on their womanhood."

"You mentioned earlier that four of your sons were married and you now have four grandchildren. Do any of their wives work outside the home?"

"Yes, two of them work, and two of them stay home."

"Which are the happier, the ones out working or the ones

staying home?"

"Oh, the ones staying home, of course."

"Why do women go out in the world and work?"

"They've been brainwashed."

"What does that mean?" I asked.

"They have to act in these new ways and have all these new things they advertise on TV, on the radio, and in the magazines and newspapers—they have to have it all!" Now she was warming to her subject, and I led her on with...

"Any other reasons?"

"Well, in today's economy it takes just about two salaries to make it."

"What do you mean, "make it?""

"Have a home and all these things people want."

" 'All these things people want,' is that bad?"

"We've got our priorities screwed up."

"Like, maybe, too much 'keeping up with the Joneses?'"

"Yes, the way they pressure us to buy everything in sight. When I was coming up, I was part of a large family. My daddy worked hard and we always had enough to eat. But instead of always rushing out and buying new things, we made do. Actually, we were poor, but I didn't know it until one day I overheard a neighbor down the street say to another one, "You know, those people in the gray house with all those kids, they're poor."

I shared my similar experiences and feelings of my own earlier days, then asked, "Do you think you were happier then than the people you see around you today who seem to 'have it all"?'

"I surely do. It's not so much what you have as what you think you have."

At this point I reached in my briefcase and pulled out a book, *How Men Feel,* I had brought along to read. After she had glanced at the cover, I asked, "How *do* men feel these days?"

"Men don't know who they are any more."

"How so?"

"Women have lost their femininity and men are losing their masculinity. They try to open the door for a lady and she beats him to it. We are different, made different, feel different. If you read the Bible, you'll see it all there. If you buy some complex something these days, you read the directions how to use it. So read the Bible. It is the users manual for men and women to live with each other. The Bible says the man is to love and cherish and care for the woman, and the woman is to help her husband and stay with him in sickness and in health, in good times and bad. Of course, if more men would do that, more women would be happier and maybe more of them would stay home."

The "Ready" call came for her car, and as she got up to go to the window to pay her bill she said, holding out her hand, "God bless your work."

Don't walk in front of me,
I may not follow.
Do not walk behind me,
I may not lead.
Walk beside me
and just be my friend.

Albert Camus

17. Patriarchy: World "Law"

Women coming into the United States from the less developed—and even from the "more civilized" countries face a bewildering woman-man scenario.

Many (most!) come from family backgrounds rooted in patriarchy; the man is "the law." How are they to navigate the wave of feminism swirling about them? They are pulled two ways. One part of them says to look up to a man. The other, look him in the eye as an equal. This is the USA today. But in most other countries around the world, patriarchy reigns. Women are taught to look up to men, to keep their places as second class citizens.

I have worked in thirty-seven countries around the world giving lectures and workshops on the multilevel philosophy of learning and living. I experienced the extreme end of patriarchy and women's servitude in the wilds of upper Thailand, some 200 miles north of Bangkok. Here, the government had just completed a new college campus of modern buildings, literally hacked out of the jungle.

As guests of the Dean, my wife and I sat on a comfortable sofa in his quite modern home for cocktails before dinner. After brief small talk (he and his wife spoke almost perfect English) his wife snapped her fingers. With what happened next, I was plunged into a world of patriarchy and women's servitude eclipsing anything I had experienced in any country. Here they came, two young women crawling on hands and knees—two knees and one hand, the other hand holding aloft a tray of cocktails and hors d'oeuvres. In my revulsion I nearly refused to reach out for a glass. But here I was, an honored guest. Revolted or not, the game must be played.

Next day, mingling with students and professors before and after my lecture, I found the same subservient attitude among the women, but nowhere near the degree of outright degradation I had experienced the night before. I have experienced the same phenomenon in the less developed countries of Asia, Africa, and South America. In Europe, it is less noticeable, especially in the north countries, as well as in the continent of Australia. In Sweden and Iceland, women reach their political peak as presidents of their respective countries. However, in the former USSR and with the peoples bordering the Mediterranean, patriarchy is still much in evidence, as it is in Japan.

But here's a curious thing. When a woman does reach the heights of the workplace on her own merit, she has more power than women in the same position in the United States.

I experienced a high point of women's status at work in India. In Bombay, I lectured, consulted and worked with teachers and the administrative staff. Here, Dr. Madhuri Shah presided over a school system of 500,000 students. Working closely with her, I had many occasions to see her absolute, unquestioned authority over her mostly male staff. And she was respected and admired by all. She had earned her way, and they all knew it. And I found this to be true in many less developed countries.

But, virtual slavery is the lot of most women in the world's poorest countries where, according to the World Bank, more than half of the world's population lives.

Education is systematically withheld from women. Only 41 percent of girls in these low-income countries are enrolled in primary school; in some cultures, fewer than a third. These decisions are made by men. Too often, women's experiences are like those cited by Dr. Janice Jiggins in her new book, *Changing Boundaries*. In Chotanapur, in Ranchi, India, women are not even allowed to attend meetings affecting the community. "The men say—bhago [go away] if we go near...what do women know about these matters...women are not buddiman [endowed with intelligence]."

So how do women, coming to Western culture from such dark-age backgrounds, relate to a man, love a man—men in general? For that matter, how do women born into our own culture respond to their instinctive feminine needs? How are they to address themselves to a society in the gender turmoil of our present United States of America?

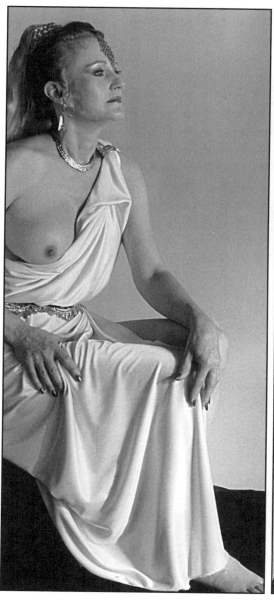

POWER:

Women had it, lost it
~ and now?

18. POWER: Women Had It, Lost It —And Now?

In ancient times women, through their Goddesses, controlled the temple, the political scene and sex. Some say it began as far back as 30,000 B.C. Archeological digs have brought up small figurines made of stone and bone and clay, now referred to as *Venus figures,* often found placed in niches or hollow places in walls of the first crude houses as objects for special consideration and attention. Found in areas extending from present-day British Isles, across Europe and into Russia, these "goddess" figures spanned a period of thousands of years. In her book, *The Language of the Goddess* (HarperSan Francisco, 1989), Marija Gimbutas has traced the rise of the Goddess concept through the many cultures of the Paleolithic and Neolithic Ages, the Bronze Age and the Iron Age with implications for today's "civilizations."

Worship of woman came naturally. Tracing the development of civilization up through the centuries, we find that it was woman who organized the home to grow the corn, comb the wool, make the pottery, cook the food, and design the tools. While men were out chasing wild animals for food, women created a life-style that was to produce flourishing cultures. "Women, in fact, invented industrialization," wrote Buckminster Fuller. And women put men to work.

As women gained control over the stuff of life, so they increasingly influenced the concept of life and death, and Goddess religion became the focus of worship, filling human need for a power larger than itself. And in those days it was easy for men to accept Goddess worship. They knew that only women could perform the magic of bringing forth a child. Only centuries later did men connect the sex act as their part in creating new life. Even today, in some primitive societies, men are still unaware of their paternity power.

Goddess worship reached a pinnacle in the flourishing cultures of Sumer, Babylon, Egypt and other areas of the Middle East. Goddess mythology gives numerous accounts of female Creators not only of peoples but of all the earth and the heavens above. Great temples were raised in their honor. Priestesses gathered followers and took lovers among the men of the community. Sensuality became sacred and sexuality an experience of the divine. Women of the times were privileged to take two husbands and often did. Women enjoyed their sexuality and the creativity thereof not only in bearing children but in the fields of art, music and literature. Written language discovered at the temple of the Queen of Heaven, was first pressed into clay by women three thousand years before Christ. Women provided political leadership for city-states and sailed their mariners over far-flung seas. Yet woman retained her nurturing qualities and her connection with psychic power that gave her foresight, insight and intelligence unique to woman.

Things were going well for women. Then came the male-oriented Indo-European invaders, riding rough-shod over "the cradle of civilization" as we have come to know the highly developed Goddess culture of the Middle East. Their fierce two-abreast horse drawn chariots and iron weapons easily overpowered the softer Bronze Age defenses of the Goddess cultures. But things were not all that bad, and their influence among the female population increased. Some anthropologists say the larger penises of the meat eaters from the North were more to the liking of the women of the time. But the invaders were also genuinely influenced by those whom they conquered, and Goddess worship continued.

Perhaps the Golden Age of Greece, followed by the halcyon days of the Roman Empire saw the peak of Goddess worship. Personified by Artemis (Roman, Diana), Athena (Minerva), Hestia (Vesta), Hera (Juno), Demeter (Ceres), Persephone (Proserpina), Aphrodite (Venus) and lesser Goddesses, it continued for nearly four centuries after Christ when, in A.D.380, Emperor Theodosias, despising the religion of women, closed down the temples of the Goddesses in Rome. But even for hundreds of years before, men had been tearing down Goddess temples, smashing Goddess images and doing all manner of religious, political and sexual acts to "put woman in her place."

The beginning of the end of Goddess worship and woman's power occurred in early biblical times, somewhere around five hundred years before Christ. Now the Levite priests began in earnest to wrest control of the temple, politics and sex from woman by using the story of Adam and Eve, branding her a sinner to be controlled by man.

"She made me do it," Adam told God when he put the question: "Hast thou eaten of the tree whereof I commanded thee that thou shouldest not eat?" (Gen. 3:11-12). Isn't it interesting that these early creators of the Bible put the blame on woman? Could they not have just as easily reversed the situation: Eve sorrowfully telling the Lord, "He made me do it," thus turning man into the sinner? But this would not have accomplished the purpose of the Levite priests who saw clearly that their power depended on establishing quickly and firmly the idea of male superiority. Why, a man wouldn't do such a thing!

Fertile ground for establishing a whole new cult of masculinity, the wandering tribes of the Hebrews, though numbering few, nevertheless succeeded in setting themselves firmly over women.

Another master stroke of the Levites was the stressing of One God as opposed to the many Goddesses worshiped by women and the men of the times. One God gave them the concentration of power they needed to lure people into wanting a piece of that One Big Power—the power only the priests could communicate with and thus tell the people what The Power, God, wanted them to do.

In the name of the new God, and demanding fire sacrifices ("burnt offerings" the Bible calls them) of the tribes of Israel, the Levite priests garnered not only a good living but luxury, created by the sweat of the Hebrew brow. The Bible tells of one such offering (Num.1:84-88) which netted the priests "silver vessels worth 2,400 shekels, 120 shekels in gold, 36 bulls, 72 full-grown rams, 72 he-goats and 72 yearling rams" to be brought to the "Tent of the Presence," ...for it was he (the priest) whom the Lord God chose from all the tribes to attend on the Lord (Deut.18:2-8). As the sons of Levi consolidated their power, they drove the women from the temple, destroyed most of their images and set about subjugating woman according to the word of God: "...thy desire shall be to thy husband and he shall rule over thee." (Gen.4:16).

The Judeo-Christian religion enabled men to extend their power over women, taking form in far flung churches through the world and lasting over the past two thousand years.

How unfortunate that the Holy Bible of the Christian religion, while so often dispensing wisdom and beauty, has been used to put woman down rather than reflect Christ's Golden Rule in man-woman relationships. If men had been "doing unto others as they would that others did unto them" in their treatment of women over the centuries, would there be a woman's movement today?

19. POWER: Taking It Back

Today, woman is working her way back into control of the temple, politics and sex—from the city council, to the corporate board room to the Senate chamber and, in Norway and Iceland, to the presidency of her country. And it's all happening so fast. In ancient times woman's rise to power occurred over centuries. Whereas it took fast runners a week to deliver a message on foot a few hundred miles, today the message is flashed around the world in seconds!

Electronic communication has turned our vast Planet Earth into a global village where news travels faster than walking next door. Result: Women everywhere are able to become aware of each other's thoughts and actions literally while they're happening. No longer do they feel "it's only us" here in our little group, our city, our state or our nation. They are feeling the surge of the women's movement, reinforcing each other around the world in the drive for equal power with men now, and into the 21st Century.

The awakening of the sleeping giantess is confirming the worst fears of men: the more education they get, the more power they want. The old saying among men, "keep 'em barefoot and pregnant" is no longer working. As their ability to read and think and question has increased, it has seemed strange to woman that the wise and loving God portrayed in the Bible could be so in favor of putting down one-half of His human creation, women, while exalting the male half.

In her book, *The Once and Future Goddess* (HarperSan Francisco, 1989), Elinor Gadon illuminates a new day. Quoting:

> Our new understanding of female sexuality based on psychological and physiological re-search that was in part engendered by the nagging questions of the women's movement demonstrates that for women the organs of sexuality and reproduction are distinct. Although sexual activity can lead to pro-creation, this is not most women's usual motivation. Our sexual life is far more encompassing, closely related to our most intimate relationships. Sexual/erotic desire for most women is seated in the clitoris as well as the vagina, a quite separate organ, the vehicle for the transmission of the male seed necessary for conception. Human females are unique among primates in that their sexual desire is not determined by their fertility cycle.... The blurring of the distinctions inherent in patriarchy between male and female sexuality has obscured this important fact.

With their newly acquired work skills, earning power and birth control, women are finding new meanings in the words "love" and "choice": love, sex, motherhood—all three, or none of the above. Kathy Keeton, President and Co-Founder of *Omni* magazine, the world's leading consumer science magazine has written a book, *Women of Tomorrow*. Here she lists ten different ways a woman can have a child without actually having sexual contact with a man. Women need relatively few men to carry on the race. Men need many more women to fulfill their paternity power—not to mention their sex drive.

So how are men reacting to all this? Much depends on the age and status of the man. But a growing concern, even a subconscious fear, is surfacing among the male population. Younger men with less status are apt to react with violence and rape. Older men with status have other ways of dealing with their growing fears like blocking job promotion, demanding sex as "part of the job" and, in more subtle ways, seeking to retain their power *over* instead of feeling fortunate to have woman's equal (and sometimes superior) intelligence and often greater insights to achieve power *with* her. And sometimes, of course, men are retreating into homosexuality or simply suffering impotency in silence, leaving women to wonder what is going on. At the other end of the gender spectrum, women give up on men and turn to lesbianism.

If men and women were to consolidate their unique powers as male and female instead of engaging in "the battle of the sexes," or retreating from a unique opportunity for mutual benefit, there would be plenty of excitement and feelings of accomplishment for both. A fledgling "mom and pop" business may grow into a huge enterprise. Or it may remain a cozy little operation that lets each one do her/his thing and have more of life's goodness for both, loving and sharing all the way.

In the late 1890's, Marie and Pierre Curie, as man and wife, worked together discovering radioactivity and radium. In 1903, the Nobel Prize for Physics was awarded jointly to the two who had worked together over the years, each maintaining their own integrity yet sharing their scientific powers to achieve power *with* each other, never power *over.* Result: each got more by seeking power *with* each other than they would have by seeking power *over* the other to grab the whole pie, since each developed a piece of the answer. As it turned out they shared equally in the $290,000 prize.

Women who are demonstrating their "can do" in every kind of job and profession, and men who are accepting the unique ways in which woman can help create a better world are the people of the future. A new breed of man is now arising who can literally "cash in" on what woman has to offer both in the workplace as well as in the "heartplace."

As a man of 83, married more than once and experiencing women in both places, I can say, "Women, look around you. There *are* such men, and they might be of any age. Though relatively few now, their numbers are growing and they are learning to embrace your total womanhood in body-mind-spirit as a comrade-in-arms, going forth to meet and deal with everyday ups and downs, and weave dreams of a future together in which each delights in the other's growth into the best possible human."

20. Why Not A Partnership Society?

A major goal of this book is to help you and women everywhere in the awesome task of literally selling men on the need for changing our dominator culture to a partnership society. You can do it by helping men to break through their own culture-bound armor of non-feeling that makes them perpetuate the dominator culture. They simply cannot *feel* where you are. Or can they—and simply won't admit it? It wouldn't be "masculine."

How can you help? You can let them know that you know that inside that armor lie feelings as caring and as nurturing as those attributed mainly to women. Some men have actually chosen careers that let them express these feelings as a way of life. The Army or Navy hospital corpsmen caring for and often risking their lives for their buddies, on the battlefield or aboard a stricken ship, are examples. Physicians, male as well as female, surely have a large measure of the caring "instinct." Men have hurled themselves into treacherous waters to save a life, sometimes at the cost of their own.

Men *can* embrace the concept of the life-giving chalice instead of the destructive blade. In his search for the Holy Grail, Sir Galahad, the fabled knight of Arthurian legends, went about the country doing noble deeds and spreading acts of kindness and caring to all about him. He was also greatly respected for his physical prowess when needed to right a wrong or free the oppressed. Feeling the need to take care of another human being comes as naturally to a man as to a woman. But the dominator culture has too often cut a man off from his true feelings! It has happened to me, more than once. I have found that women help us to claim our real feelings!

What can you, a woman, do to help men turn from dominator destructiveness of each other and of the Great Mother Earth Goddess to a co-nurturing partnership with women, with each other, and with Planet Earth? You can use your Goddess Power to help us feel masculine about using our own caring powers, using our strengths to fight the destruction of Mother Earth. The ecological warriors of Greenpeace, risking life and limb, are an example. Those who fight for equal rights for women, blacks, Hispanics, Asians and other minorities, are other examples.

The conqueror writes the history. Hitler re-wrote Germany's history to "prove" the Aryan race superior. Stalin re-wrote Russia's history to "show" that communism was the only way to go, and so on, back down the centuries.

About 5,000 years ago, men wielding the blade and the masculine dominator principle swept down from Northern Europe to conquer a peaceful, chalice-oriented civilization in what we now call the Middle East. Here flourished a social order based on a feminine principle carefully balanced with the masculine principle and symbolized by the nourishing cup of life, the Chalice. Religion and the way of life was based on respect for the Great Goddess Mother Earth, Gaia.

Out of appreciation for the Great Mother's gifts of food, clothing, and shelter came the worship of several Goddesses. Each Goddess represented different aspects of humans' relationships with the Mother Goddess and with each other.

Honor for woman, from whom life flowed to create new human beings came naturally. Goddess worship fostered a creative, co-nurturing partnership between women and men which lasted for over twenty centuries, somewhere between 7,000 and 4,500 B.C. The Chalice flourished. Then came the "Blade."

The "murder" of this remarkably advanced and peaceful Chalice culture by the men of the Blade is now being documented by delving into the secrets of women's history. Facts ignored or at best treated casually by the history writers, men, for the past 5,000 years, are now being revealed.

A most powerful expose of this cover-up is Riane Eisler's *The Chalice And The Blade* (Harper and Row, 1987). In her devastating but fascinating book, the author documents the several re-writes history has undergone at the hands of male-dominated religious orders and warrior-kings to assure the continued domination by the male half of the world's people over the female half. Through her years of ground-breaking research and perceptive insights, Eisler projects history into the future: By performing a cultural transformation from a dominator culture to a partnership social order we can not only survive but gain the good things of life for women and men the world over. Will we recognize and use the energies of Goddess Power to make this transformation, or will we let the dominator culture continue to foist the fiction of its success upon us?

What is Goddess Power?

Goddess Power is, first of all, something every woman has because she is a woman. It is the unique power, strength and set of characteristics possessed by one-half of the world's population. But the full realization of *your* own unique

Goddess Power can only come by knowing ever more deeply the Seven Goddesses within *you*. What's more, the infinite range of goddess characteristics you can call upon enables you to learn what you really want, and how to get it—and to be more of the woman you want to be.

Goddess Power is *not* the power to control, to command, to be supreme, or to dominate as men have taken power to themselves over the past thousands of years. Symbol: The Blade.

Goddess Power is the unique strength, quality, and set of characteristics possessed by one-half of the world's population. These attributes are nourishing, life-sustaining and identified with birth and growth of plant, animal, and human life. Symbol: The Chalice.

According to *Webster's Dictionary*: "Power may imply latent or exerted physical, mental or spiritual ability to act or be acted on. Force implies the actual and efficacious exercise of power. Energy applies to power expended, or capable of being transformed into work. Strength applies to the quality or property of a person or thing that enables him (and her, Mr. Webster!) to exert force or withstand strain, pressure, or attack." Each of these attributes: power, force, energy, and strength define Goddess Power and the potential of women to find these qualities within themselves.

Perhaps the most exciting thing about Goddess Power is that you have a seven-fold force at your command. Take counsel with each of your Seven Goddesses; meditate on the strengths of each. Envision how they can help you not only in improving your own life, but to express your highest calling as a creator and conserver of life with a mission and a message to patriarchy, changing from power *over* to power *with*.

21. Do Men Fear Women?

☐ *All?*
  ☐ *Many?*
    ☐ *Some?*
      ☐ *A few?*
        ☐ *Your man?*

I have never had these feelings about women. I have feared some men. But according to Author Anthony Astrachan in his 1986 book, *How Men Feel, (Anchor Press/Doubleday),* many of the 400 men he interviewed, in all walks of life, do have fear of women and the increasing power of the women's movement. I believe that were I now, say, 30 to 45 or 50 (instead of 83) I might be sharing these same feelings.

Beyond his personal interviews, Astrachan looked at how men are responding to the changing scenario in man-woman relationships as reflected in TV, the theatre, films, books and periodical literature. He found a shift in men's attitudes beginning in the early 1970's and extending through the Reagan era. Throughout, there is dramatic evidence of men's

hostility toward women. While some men feel relief, admiration, identification and pleasure in "the new woman," the negatives —fear, anxiety, envy and shame often outweigh the positives. As a result, instead of accepting woman's increasing show of competence and achievement and women as peers, at home and in the workplace, men are still more likely to hold on to their old perceptions of women as wives and lovers, madonnas and whores; daughters, mothers, sisters. But in spite of the building backlash, the book's author feels that the sexual revolution will progress, though slowly, as small but increasing numbers of men show support for women's efforts to change their lives, and consequently, their own.

So what is going to happen to maintain or even speed up the progress of men's acceptance of the new demands of women? Will it take changes in the workplace—flexible time, job-sharing, etc. to allow men to have more time at home for co-parenting and sharing in homemaking chores? The number of men who respond to such opportunities will no doubt increase, but the trend will be bucking centuries of male dominance viewpoint: child care and housekeeping is "women's work." Men's work—except for a "Mister Fix-it" role

and a little lawn mowing, etc.—is outside the home. Further, he is to come home after a hard day's work, put his feet up and rest. In Russia, where 80 percent of women work, the "Mr. Mom" idea is even more unthinkable. The problem seems international. Will a new breed of superwoman arise who can find the energy for both workplace and home? Will man find another planet—or become extinct!

For at least five thousand years, men have developed a dominator culture in which one-half of the world's population—men, dominated the other half of all human beings on earth—women. Men have been carefully taught to carry on and even expand this way of thinking and acting. And even though what men (and women) have been sold as "masculine" values—might makes right, conquer and rule—are not working, these dominator values still persist.

Will change have to wait until we blow ourselves up, leaving nothing to change? Will it have to wait until we have used up or destroyed the fragile and dwindling resources of Mother Earth? Will we have to wait until "leadership" centers in the hands of so few we find ourselves living in a police state—George Orwell's *The World of 1984*, whether we call it the (former) USSR or the USA? The continuance of dominator culture can only hurry us toward these sordid "goals."

What can you, as a woman, do to transform the social order, worldwide, from a dominator culture—man *over* woman, to a partnership culture—women *with* men as co-nourishing equals?

Use your Goddess Power!

Women can learn how to re-introduce to the world the ancient and durable respect for and worship of Gaia, the Great Mother Earth Goddess. How? By knowing and activating the Seven Goddesses within her, a woman can begin to exert her Goddess Power. And she can encourage other women to do the same, *and* help men to see and learn their parts in the cultural transformation that must take place. The alternative is unthinkable: The end of life on earth, quickly, with the "blade" (read "Bomb") or slowly and painfully as the "blade" saws slowly into human liberty and the life-giving resources of Mother Earth. Women, by their very nature, can give us the ecological and bio-social leadership we need for survival. Outstanding is Dr. Helen Caldecott in her book *If You Love This Planet.*

I own and have read or scanned nearly a hundred books by or about women. An attempt to summarize would be awesome. However, I believe that the essence of those powerful writers goes something like this:

> Women are discovering a new mission to mankind. Increasingly, she feels it in all her collective rage, sadness and joy in being a woman. Bearing life into the world and sustaining that life, she has always treasured her image as both creator and protector of life. But now, a new awakening, a new "assignment."
>
> It is becoming eloquently clear that women must help man to experience heart-opening changes, releasing him from his "stand-and-deliver," "stiff-upper-lip" stance into feeling the *anima* within him as well as the *animus.* C. G. Jung has said that in every man resides a female energy, the *anima*. In like manner, side by side with a woman's *anima,* her pervasive feminine nature, there lives the *animus*, the masculine.

In helping men to round out their lives by discovering the *anima* within, women will, in no way —as so many men seem to fear— rob them of their manhood. Instead, they will elevate the masculine *animus* to higher co-creation of love, sexuality and emotional richness. Women are now taking on this high and holy mission. It is now time for men (including me!) to listen up. If we fail to put away our fears and take this next big step for mankind, we will imperil our existence on Planet Earth. I believe that a "critical mass" of woman-man energy is shaping up to change world culture toward humankind's next higher level.

It may be insane
to live in a dream.
But it is madness
to live without one.

Author Unknown

22. Make Love – Not War!

Make love–not war!

Why didn't we think of this before? The ancient Greeks did!

In 411 B.C., about two thousand four-hundred years ago, the Greek playwright, Aristophanes, presented his drama, *Lysistrata*. While his creation appealed to the comic side of his audience, the assumption that women, by a determined and concerted action of withholding sex from men could effect peace and governmental reform is not exactly funny.

The Second Peloponesian War between Athens and Sparta was raging, and Lysistrata, a prominent Athenian woman torn asunder by the useless destruction, hit upon a desperate idea. Women create life, men kill it. Women give men the one thing they seem unable to do without: Sex. Withhold sex and you can get what you want. If all women said "No more sex until you stop the wars," they would stop.

Lysistrata went over to Sparta, the enemy, and talked with Lampito, a prominent woman of her country. "Yes," she said, "why not? Are not all women alike in not wanting their children, homes and cities destroyed? We women must join together!" And, indeed, finally all women joined in the movement.

While some of the younger women weakened, enough "no sex" prevailed to bring even the generals to their knees. "My men cannot go on fighting without the relief from their stresses and the rejuvenation of their bodies through having sex with a woman!"

As a last straw, a lovely, nude young woman, representing the goddess of peace, was brought before a vast gathering of soldiers in a field between the two cities. The sex-starved men, their eyes devouring the nude maiden, was too much. Their leaders knew they were beaten and sent emissaries to the women to talk terms. Not until the generals had gone over the parchment scrolls, agreeing to each word and signing the papers ceremoniously did the women open their arms to their husbands and sweethearts, whereupon all departed hastily for home—and bed!

MEN! We put you on notice:
NO MORE SEX,
>   ***no more love-making until***
>   ***you stop making war!***

We women go through the hell of birth pangs, almost unbearable, we nurture your babies, we bring up your children, THEN YOU KILL THEM. NO MORE SEX UNTIL YOU STOP THE KILLING!

Can we do it, girls?

(Audience) *Y-e-e—s-s-s!*

Politics hasn't done it, our "leaders" haven't done it, the UN hasn't done it. We women have got to do it!

(Voice) *OK, we can do it, but what about the women of Russia, and all the other countries?]*

Aren't we all women? Don't we all suffer the same birth pangs and nurture our children only to see them grow up to be hurled at one another to be killed?

(Voice) *How do we get to them?*

Infiltrate! We go and talk with them, the women, not just of our so-called enemies, but all women of the world.

They're just like us.

(Another voice) *I know several in Russia. I've just been there.*

(More voices) *I know women in England and Nicaragua. I know three women in China I can talk to. I have women friends in India. They'd listen up!*

(The audience buzz grows into a din as excited voices tell of ways of contacting the women of the world)

(Voice) *What will the men do with themselves without wars to make weapons for, make plans for, and fight? Let the men use their armies and navies to build beautiful cities in wide open spaces for people in a world where two-thirds are living in hunger and poverty.*

(Audience) *Y-e-e-a-a-a!*

OK, girls, are we strong enough, dedicated enough, to do without sex ourselves?

(Voices) *I am! Sure! It won't be easy, but I'll do it! etc.*

(Another voice) *What about prostitutes?*

(Another voice) *We'll raise a fund to take care of them, help them find jobs.*

(Another voice) *When do we begin with our NO SEX? What do you say, girls, when? Tomorrow? next week? tonight?*

(Audience roars) *To-n-i-i-gh-gh-t!*

Chapter 23. What's Holding Up The Parade?

What's really holding up the progress toward accepting and acting on the conserving, life-giving feminine principle? Men, of course. But, as we shall see, women themselves, many of them, are often consciously or subconsciously, doing things that make men want to possess their bodies and little else.

Snapshot: Male View

Out of the corner of my eye, seated comfortably in the great room, a motion, a female hand seeking to hide her body consciousness—crossed legs, skirt mid-thigh, from her subconscious (conscious!) sense of the male quest for hidden treasures—hers (and mine!)

The Executive Director of Planned Parenthood—dealing with the activities of such things in younger and more vulnerable generations, spoke to an attentive audience of 50 quite mature adults, intent on seeing how well our contributions were spent. Absorbing, intellectual. Yet, there, she did it again. The ever so slight tugging on the tight skirt to cover what she fancied was the exposure of her womanhood.

Fairly well formed, in her 40's-50's, I assessed her desirability and found it wanting. And yet—and yet, I found myself being satisfied, actually proud she was a woman, and I, a man, and that she shared here the concerns that recognized my maleness and signified her sensualness. Here is the way our creator made us. And, happily, at age 83, I can still live, for even a moment, in the feelings that have powered the peopling of Planet Earth, and give thanks for being a player, in the Grand Scheme of Things. Getting there with Goddess Power!

Men 🧍🧍🧍🧍🧍🧍🧍🧍🧍 design dresses

SEARS,ROEBUCK&CO.,INC. women buy them

so they can wear them to attract

men 🧍🧍🧍🧍🧍🧍🧍🧍🧍

1897 to take them off*

(Hasn't *any*thing changed?)

* From the libreto, *Size 12*, by Mary Scott, from the musical, *Size 12*, by Mary Scott and David Glover, 1986.

So what is holding up the parade of women toward more equality: Men wanting to dominate women, or women wanting to be "taken?" Men, these days, are more than slightly confused. On the one hand, women rally for "equality" and against male domination while, on the other, doing everything in their power to attract men, inviting their "capture."

"A sexy woman lets her man feel that she is his private property," advises an article in COSMOPOLITAN Magazine, February, 1995, a magazine that delights in "telling it all." The "Cosmo Girl" gracing the cover of each month's issue leads women into page after page of advertisements touting the latest cosmetics and fashions practically guaranteeing to turn a woman into a mouth-watering, irresistible siren for men. "The sleekest, rubberized slip dress, to make Valentine's heart pound," says one. "Not just hot, but sizzling," says another of "seriously shiny leggings." "Three steps to sexy" in mid-riff baring tops "for your after-dark life." "A fragrance so sensual even the French were shocked."

Women will even endure pain to be attractive to men. As Margaret Carlson writes in the April 4, 1994, TIME magazine:

> The latest instruments of female torture are
> contraptions with names like Wonderbra
> and Super-Uplift that force a woman's breasts,
> however small, into a harness, creating
> cleavage of the sort enjoyed by Dolly Parton....
>
> When Super-Uplift went on sale at Man-
> hattan's Saks Fifth Avenue, 489 were bought
> the first day....

There is a postfeminist argument for the Wonderbra: liberation means that women can dress any way they want. No more the little bow tie and the boxy gray suit or the Sears orthopedically correct underwear beneath it. Women should feel free to be sexy in the boardroom as well as the bedroom. But then the message becomes: Notice my breasts before you notice my recommendation to go long on pork-belly futures...

Are men ignoring it all? Can a man go against nature? And the higher they go in the business world, the more men act on their appreciation for what women are putting out there. In one issue, COSMOPOLITAN magazine went right to the top with no-holds-barred questions to several of these boardroom power brokers about their sex lives.

"Powerful men: Are They As Good In the Bedroom As They Are in The Boardroom?" headlines the article by Michael Segell. The subtitle: "Maybe better! CEOs, arbitrageurs, media moguls, political movers and shakers, go after pleasure like the overachievers they are." During the interview, Segell's notebook recorded the feelings of these men "right out of the horse's mouth." One acknowledged, "There's no question that success changes your sexual view. I'm not sure why, but it increases your appetite—and your ability to indulge that appetite." Another boardroom buddy: "The boys running the fashion and cosmetics industries—like bulls in a cow barn." And still another: "He shoulda' gone to Washington. Submission is all the rage on the Beltway, I hear." And many more.

In the same article, we hear from women: "They're conquerors," said one woman, an art gallery owner who'd been agreeably "conquered" by several Masters of the Universe. "They've got to go to work, win every meeting of the day... then they come home and conquer *you.*

Marriage? Sometimes. "I'll tell you how I got my husband. Sex....When he knew what sex could be like, he was hooked."

In the same issue of COSMOPOLITAN, JoAnna Nicholson's article, "The Way To Be Surely, Surely Sexy," is subtitled "Want him to be totally entranced? You don't have to do anything crazy or unnatural, but these utterly practical suggestions work." Drawing on her book, *How To Be Sexy Without Looking Sleazy,* the article goes on to say that, "A sexy woman readies her man's mind and body. subtly, a little at a time, until he feels incomparable passion.

Even such at-the-checkout-counter magazines as Family Circle gets in the act with a plethora of "beauty" ads and such articles as "Doing It In The Back Seat Like You Used To" to recapture love. Equally qualified as "parade stoppers," the stores and catalogs of *Victoria's Secret* and *Frederick's of Hollywood* are devoted to around-the-clock wear for women to present their most enticingly sexy selves. Should such a catalog fall into the hands of a man, he views the contents with rising expectations.

So what's happening to the "parade?"

And now we come to sexual harassment. What do women

expect, wearing dresses "up to here" and "down to there?" Do they think men are made of wood, incapable of feeling? And if a man does respond with a look, and perhaps a casual touch as they pass by going down a hall or out a door, "Oh, I am being sexually harassed!"

And if the woman gets no male response from her display of feminine wiles: "Oh, why am I spending all this money for clothes, cosmetics and jewelry?"

So what's a poor woman to do? What's a poor man to do? Even meeting at the water cooler may soon bring on a suit for sexual harassment.

Do men want women to "dress down," to look less attractive? This man doesn't, and I don't know any men who do. In pre-women's lib days, both sexes welcomed the brief encounter, often hoping it would turn into something more. Why the change today? Perhaps it's because the whole atmosphere is becoming so sexually charged. It's like tinder awaiting the spark to blaze. Or more like gunpowder, waiting for the trigger to be pulled by either woman or man. Why can't we "make love, not war?"

Aphrodite and Persephone now seem to have taken over the scene. When will Goddess Athena, with her cool wisdom, begin to turn the center stage spotlight more onto the life sustaining, family-building Goddesses Hestia, Hera and Demeter? Or should a woman call more on Artemis for the strength of self-suffering to simply live without men? As for men, classes in "How to Be A Gentleman In Spite of It All" would not be amiss.

Actually, it's up to each woman to decide which Goddess she wants to put out front and to deal with whatever response she gets. Some women even go so far as to turn their bodies into skeletons in the belief this fashion-runway image will attract a man. Especially among those younger, anorexic and bulimic behaviors, painful as they are to themselves and to those around them, are on the rise. If they will listen to their Goddess Consciousness they will not let themselves be driven to such death-inviting behavior to satisfy their imbalance of Persephone-Aphrodite energy.

So
What's
new
?

24. Why Be A Skeleton?

Get off your
HUNGER STRIKE!
Throw off the chains of
anorexia/bulimia

- **Break the power of the men (and the women) who are starving your body-mind-spirit to death!**

- **Get out of the clutches of the multi-billion dollar fashion, cosmetic and weight-loss industries!**

—not to mention the tobacco, soaps, and other less obviously connected business billions. These people prey like vultures on the anorexic, or near-anorexic woman. If you don't have the disease, they'll give it to you through their high-powered advertising on TV, radio, in magazines, newspapers or mailboxes-full of catalogs.

And Wall Street pyramids profits on you. It is as though one part of the culture is cannibalizing the other, literally eating the flesh off your bones.

By persisting in thin-ness you are proving nothing but your inability to handle your conflict between desperately wanting sex and rejecting it; between affirming your woman-ess and denying it. Get help from your friends, or a therapist. Or, you can do it *yourself!* You have Goddess Power.

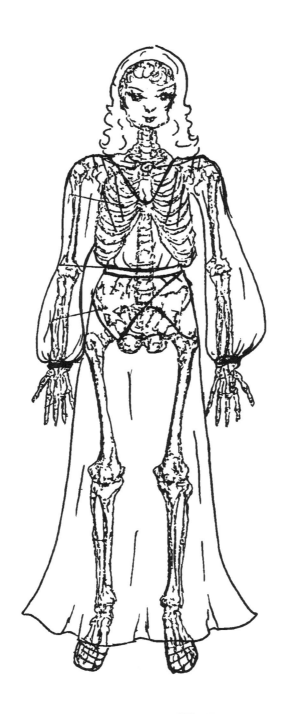

I like to have a real woman in my arms — not a scarecrow

Real men appreciate the full, richly rounded body of a *real* woman. Down through the centuries, famous paintings and sculptures have glorified the generously formed female. And these works were created by men. Would men buy PLAYBOY MAGAZINE if the centerfold were a bag of bones?

Some men, mainly macho types, seem to be attracted to thin, weak-looking women, thinking them easy to control. But what they find underneath that supple, willowy exterior is likely to be just the opposite: a woman of steel, driven by the rigid discipline that has made it possible to deny herself food she so craved, in the name of self-control. Instead of the soft, compliant creature she would like to appear to be, she is more like a coiled spring ready to leap out and strike from a position of desperation and even a burning hatred of men whom she secretly accuses of being responsible for her plight. So, her shapeless, bony body sheathed in seductive black, neckline cut down to her navel —since she had so little else to show, the anorexic lures men like moth to flame, reducing them to pawns, and starving herself, at times, to death.

Women need to know that the image of woman as a soft, "mothering" body is still a healthy, normal man's ideal, as it always has been, and let their bodies reflect the generosity of a fully developed body-mind-spirit.

Can you imagine why so many women starve themselves into skin and bones—and think we like them that way!

This painting hangs in the world's greatest museum of art: THE HERMITAGE, St. Petersburg, Russia

MEN! *Suppose YOU*
were expected to go on a
HUNGER STRIKE
to become culturally acceptable (especially to women!)

Suppose YOU suffered from anorexia nervosa, the disease that made you feel—like so many thousands of women feel today—that your body took up too much space, that you should do everything possible to make it thinner, even at the risk of your health—even if you died from it?

Suppose women designed clothes for you that made you look thin and made you believe that "Thin is in" so you'd wear them. No more manly, boxy padded-shouldered jackets. No more bold masculine attributes you see in advertising featuring your underpants. You might even find ways to look like a virile male, but when it came to the sex act, forget it. You don't have the power.

How long would you stand for this brainwashing that the thinner you are the better man you are? Not long. You'd wake up some morning and tell them all "Go to hell! I'm going to eat; eat nutritious food, get my strength back and BE A MAN!"

So why don't you help women stop kidding themselves that you want a bag of bones instead of a luscious Playboy centerfold, or a Marilyn Monroe or any of the womanly women idolized in art and literature over the centuries. You have within you the ancient wisdom of a real man to do it. What are you waiting for?

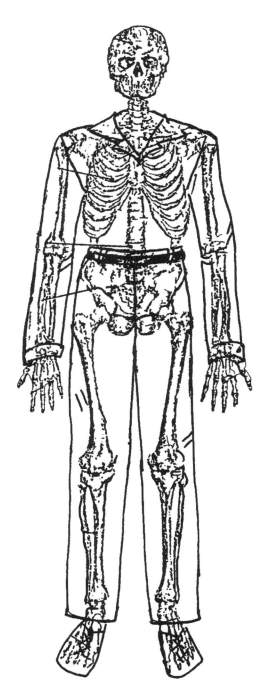

25. Are Women and Men Really Different?

"...male and female created He them."

Women's typical responses

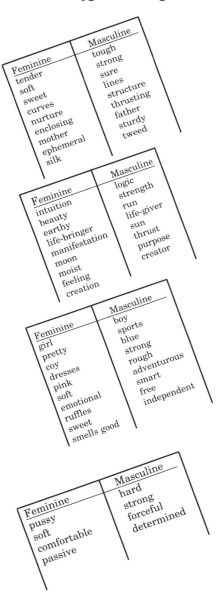

Feminine	Masculine
tender	tough
soft	strong
sweet	sure
curves	lines
nurture	structure
enclosing	thrusting
mother	father
ephemeral	sturdy
silk	tweed

Feminine	Masculine
intuition	logic
beauty	strength
earthy	run
life-bringer	life-giver
manifestation	sun
moon	thrust
moist	purpose
feeling	creator
creation	

Feminine	Masculine
girl	boy
pretty	sports
coy	blue
dresses	strong
pink	rough
soft	adventurous
emotional	smart
ruffles	free
sweet	independent
smells good	

Feminine	Masculine
pussy	hard
soft	strong
comfortable	forceful
passive	determined

I obtained dozens of responses such as you see here by always carrying a few 3 x 5 cards in my pocket. On meeting a friend, and often, a stranger, I would take out two cards, write "feminine" and "masculine" across the top, draw a line down the middle, hand the person a pen and say, "Here's a little game. Just write the first word that comes into your mind under each heading. And I'll do the same." Then we'd talk about what we wrote. Men enjoyed the game as well as women. And we learned so much! You, as did I, will find this approach a unique and appreciated way of getting acquainted. Try it! Have fun with it at a party, too. A great mixer!

As I began to collect these cards from women and men, a similarity in

Viva la difference!
YIN YANG

woman   *man*
female   *male*
feminine   *masculine*

their responses began to come through. To check my own observations, I asked others to go through a sampling of the cards for any remarkable likenesses or differences they may see. They, too, discovered that the way women viewed feminine and masculine qualities were much the same as men's description of feminine and masculine attributes. To both women and men, women are typically soft, tender, nurturing, feeling while men are strong, tough, adventurous, purposeful. Oversimplified, of course. But the Yin Yang, the play of opposites, is very real to both women and men. The sample cards displayed here show a creative range of refinement in the description each gender has of the other. No doubt, many women and men will continue to treasure these differences. Others may choose unisex.

Men's typical responses

Feminine	Masculine
weak on surface	strong on surface
gentle	kind
soft	protector
strong underneath	the father
curves	wage earner
lips	muscles
homemaker	heroes journey
breasts	penis
the enveloper	the penetrator

Comparing these responses of men with those of women, one sees that men's view of women and women's view of themselves are very much alike: Women and men are different. Broadly put, to both women and men, women are typically soft, tender, nurturing, feeling while men are strong, tough, protecting, powerful.

Feminine	Masculine
more loving	mate beater
schemer	tends to cruelty
happy in status quo	planner
latent strength	power hungry
sinks roots	hunter
life preserving	scientific
child raiser	spacially oriented

Feminine	Masculine
beauty, inner & outer	leadership
love	organizer
competence	fixer
strength	physical
especially moral foresight	

If men and women were more alike would things be better? If the magnetism of Yin Yang were removed, what would happen to the human race? Not to mention the joy of sexual fulfillment!

Feminine	Masculine
tender-tough	soft - hard
lady	gentleman
round	angular
cavern	peak
avocado	banana
cuddle	cuddler
nourishing	providing
seed bed	sower
mysterious	probing

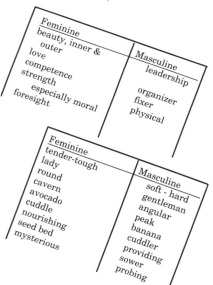

Some find women and men so alike*

Feminine	Masculine
gentle	gentle
caring	caring
tender	tender
loving	loving

Feminine	Masculine
strong	strong
fun	fun
loving	loving
true	true
creative	creative
artistic	artistic
versatile	versatile
imaginative	imaginative

*These two respondents actually wrote identical words under each heading.

Some women are disenchanted with men

Feminine	Masculine
sweet	sour
passive	aggressive
faithful	unfaithful

Feminine	Masculine
realistic	infantile
practical	idealistic
nurturing	selfish
understanding	egotistical

Femaleness	Maleness
Patience	Impatience
Broadmindedness/scope	Decisiveness
Flexibility	Singlemindedness
Competitiveness (suppressed)	Competitiveness (outward)
Outward softness(phys) /Inner strength	Outward strength (phys)/Emotional vulnerability
Perspective	Direction
Restricted:	Encouraged:
Parentally	To experiment
Financially	To succeed
Socially	To diversify
To be subdued	To be aggressive

26. All In Your Genes?

Is it true that "Anatomy is Destiny?" Is it true, for example, that the brain of a woman is different than that of a man? Will it be true, therefore, that the sex of your brain will determine how you think and act as you go through life? In an article of that title appearing in the Association for Humanistic Psychology *Perspective* for August-September, 1986, psychiatrist Elizabeth Schmid Stevens points to research that there are, indeed, essential differences in the brain structure of women and men. In her opinion, the conclusions are not all in yet, but there are growing indications that such might be the case.

Whatever the final results may be, an interesting question persists: If so, why? Is female-male brain difference genetic? Was it always this way among animals, human and otherwise? Or is the difference the result of the various ways in which women and men react to the environment? It's the old question: nature or nurture?

Which came first, the chicken or the egg?

But does it really matter? Do we really have to know? What we all seem to realize is that women and men *do* feel, think and act differently—and how dull things would be if it were otherwise. Viva la difference!

In the book, *Sex and Gender,* editors Phillip Shaver and Clyde Hendrick present 328 pages devoted to pointing out differences in women and men. As to what to do about it, seventeen authors, eleven of them women, do not seem to have found out. Or, if they know, they're not telling. I say, "Enjoy!"

All in all, although no book of a few hundred pages can possibly capture everything that is happening in the study of sex and gender—around the world and in many different disciplines—this one offers an exciting and diverse sampling. Surely there are enough ideas and challenges here to keep professionals and students busy for quite some time. The chapters illustrate the kinds of contributions that feminism, and recent changes in women's circumstances and roles (hence in men's circumstances and roles), have made.

Meanwhile, we ordinary folk don't have to wait around for "further research." We can take the facts of physiological differences in women and men and use them any way we see fit to back up any feelings we may have in order to justify the way we behave, whether we are a woman or a man.

The way you are physically put together may figure strongly in the different ways you feel, think and act in your love-life, your work-life, your play-life or your parenting. Some may "lean on" differences as an excuse for not being simply a decent human being, but it doesn't have to happen to you. Here are some of the differences that do, in fact, exist between women and men.

In case you haven't noticed, the next time you walk down the street notice that, in general,

women's bodies are shaped like this– and men's like this–

women are narrow-shouldered and broad-hipped

men are broad-shouldered and narrow-hipped.

Some things are not so obvious:

When fully grown, women are 23% muscle, 25% fat.

When fully grown, men are 40% muscle, 15% fat.

In overall strength, 25% of all women are equal to the weakest of 25% of all men.

Women can achieve pound-for-pound equality in leg strength, but even with equal training, women's upper-body strength is only one-third to two-thirds that of men.

The male hormone testosterone has been found to have effects on dominance, aggression and sexual drive in both humans and other animals.

Both sexes produce the testosterone hormone in the adrenal glands, but males produce larger quantities in their testes. You'll hear "That woman has balls!" and it will be an ardent feminist praising an especially courageous and/or aggressive sister. There may be a distinct bio-physical difference between a Bella Abzug and a Marilyn Monroe.

Men are, compared with women, about six times more likely to commit murder. In every society that has kept records, males are the most violent. And males turn out to be more cruel than females.

Can women and men ever be alike? One researcher suggests that "males and females could finally become as similar as their biology allows." China actually tried to make it happen. With their baggy-panted unisex uniforms, all women and men looked pretty much alike. Look-alike clothing and many other ways of forced sameness worked for many years of the Communist Revolution and "The Great Leap Forward." However, by the time I got to The People's Republic of China in 1980, flowered blouses and skirts had begun to blossom here and there as the female of the species began to demand her right to feel and look more frilly, colorful, "feminine." But not all women were so bold. It was not uncommon to see a baggy-panted woman and a gaily attired feminine figure walking side by side. One had "broken out." The other was clinging to the past.

Mao Tse-tung had said, "Women, being one-half of the population, must hold up their half of the sky." He may not have realized that women had been yearning for centuries to hold up their half of the sky—and get credit for it, and he didn't allow for the fact that they would want to do it differently from men. He failed to reckon with the feminine mystique. It may have cost him the revolution.

The feminine mystique is becoming less a mystery (Ah, so!) as scientists probe the brains for female-male differences. Through biofeedback and other electronic devices researchers are finding that women and men use their brains differently. For example, in the act of reading, especially in sounding out words, it was discovered that men use only a minute part of the left side of the brain while women use areas in both sides of the brain. In tests of verbal speed, women excel. In tests involving spatial relations—distances in space, imaging (what an object would look like if rotated, etc.) men excel.

For whatever reasons, it is becoming more clear that there are important differences in both the physiological and psychological attributes of women and men. What to do about it? Enjoy! *Viva la difference!*

27. Are Men From Mars? Women From Venus?

According to John Gray, Ph.D., they are. The jacket blurb for his book, *Men Are From Mars, Women Are From Venus* (Harper Collins, 1992), summarizes his thesis like this:

> ONCE UPON A TIME Martians and Venusians met, fell in love, and had happy relationships together because they respected and accepted their differences. Then they came to Earth and amnesia set in: They forgot they were from different planets.

In his book, Dr. Gray goes on to point out in great detail the differences that justify the title of his work. Among them:

MEN (Mars)	WOMEN (Venus)
Martians value power, competency, efficiency, and achievement.	Venusians value love, communication, beauty, and relationships.
"Objects," "things"	People, feelings
Practical, factual	Intuitive, sensitive
Want to solve problems alone	Want to talk openly

Throughout this very useful book, Dr. Gray catalogues the many ways in which women and men are different. He also points out how these differences become a mysterious attraction, one for the other. Their love needs can actually flow into each other. Here he summarizes the love needs of women and men:

Women need to receive	Men need to receive
1. Caring	1. Trust
2. Understanding	2. Acceptance
3. Respect	3. Appreciation
4. Devotion	4. Admiration
5. Validation	5. Approval
6. Reassurance	6. Encouragement

How to express the give and take in everyday life? Here Gray offers men "101 ways to score points with a woman" and "26 ways how women can score big with men." The lists cover several pages, each point gleaned from his study of the needs of women and men as mirrored in his own, at times turbulent, life. But he gives major credit to the over 100,000 individuals and couples who have attended his weekend workshops conducted in twenty major cities over the years. His own wife comes in for eloquent praise for her honest sharing of feminine insights and feelings.

As one who has been married more than once, I wish I had had the benefit of this book in establishing more enduring relationships. This practical "curriculum" plus a knowledge of the Seven Goddesses would have smoothed many a rocky road in both relationships and marriage.

What if...........?

What do you think?

_____

_____

_____

_____

_____

_____

28. Who Prefers Whom?

Imagine you are the Woman who wrote each one of these "Personal" ads for the National Exclaimer tabloid newspaper. Write the name of the Goddess (Artemis, Athena, Demeter, Persephone, Hera, Hestia, Aphrodite) under each ad who you think would be most likely to have written the ad to attract the kind of man she would like to meet.

Divorced, no children. Blond, 5' 2", eyes of blue, 109 lbs., lonely but lively. Attracted to older financially secure men. I can make you happy. Could you please send photo & phone?

Goddess_____

Female, 55, wants outdoor-type male, enjoy hiking, camping, companionship. Marriage? We'll see. Full photo.

Goddess_____

Secure business woman, mid-forties, seeks financially minded counterpart. It could be a nice business doing pleasure with you. Photo, phone.

Goddess_____

Wanted, best friend by mid-fifties Christian woman. Share religious experiences, cozy home. Hope you are 50-65, huggy-bear type. Long letter, please.

Goddess_____

Full-figured, emotionally healthy, newly divorced, late 30's seeks father for 2 children, 8 and 12. More if you want them. Parenting can be fun in more ways than one! Other interests, too. Write if you're Mr. Right.

Goddess_____

Attractive 30 seeks upward mobile 30-40 male who appreciates and goes after the better things in life. Social drinker, no drugs. Am one-man woman. Expect one-woman man for lifetime marriage. None other need apply. Photo.

Goddess_____

Luscious lady loves life at 45, seeks sexy man to appreciate music, dancing, the arts and all a real woman can give. Share your total manhood with me. We can make beautiful music. Exchange photos.

Goddess_____

Photographed in Russia's famous Pushkin Museum, Moscow

❂ GODDESS GAME SEVEN

Imagine you are the man who wrote each one of the "Personal" ads for the National Exclaimer tabloid newspaper. Write the name of the Goddess (Artemis, Athena, Demeter, Persephone, Hera, Hestia, Aphrodite) under each ad who would be most likely to have written the ad to attract the kind of man she would like to meet.

Recently divorced, 44, former football star, 6' 3", social drinker, no drugs, needs wife to start life over with me. Financial success gives me good things to share with right woman, 30-40. Tell me your dream. Photo please.

Goddess_____

Tired of bar scene? Me too. Ready for cozy home, Christian values, no drinking, no smoking? Me too. I'm 51, you're 45—? Phone, photo.

Goddess_____

Successful, lonely, 45, seeks brainy and beautiful partner, for exciting new business venture. Could be other ventures for right woman, 30-45. Photo.

Goddess_____

Divorced, 37, 6' 2", 210 lbs., ex-marine, nature lover, seeks active female counterpart for sailboat cruising, photography, friendship, maybe more. No children.

Goddess_____

Like the good things of life? So do I. 5' 9", good job, good dancer, like movies, dining out. Join me for fun? Late photo and "all about you."

Goddess_____

Exciting gentleman, mid-forties, 5' 9", 170 lbs., seeks jeans-to-lace lady to share the good life, have fun! Advertising agent art director, good dancer, connoisseur fine wines. And you? Tell me all. Full length front and profile. Phone.

Goddess_____

Single parent, 37, father of two, ages 6 & 8, offers good home, enough money if we both work. Let's explore interests we might share for lifetime. If you have children, consider merging families. Any nationality fine. Photos.

Goddess_____

Photographed in Russia's famous Pushkin Museum,
Moscow

29. We're All In The Same Boat

Now that it's happening—this swirling gender dance, we're all in this thing together. We're all feeling the push-pull, the stress of woman-man relationships, some more than others. As in all times of stress, feelings are intensified. Then we look around to see who-what is causing us the pain and we are most likely to take out our frustration and anger on the closest one to us—our friend, sweetheart, wife, husband, or co-worker of opposite sex on the job, depending on our own gender. One result might be the increasing deadening of all our feelings as we simply get tired of it all, turn off and tune out. Another could be open warfare, but we don't have to go through either.

Since we're all in the same boat, we have to ask and explore answers to the question: How can women and men help each other as we sail through these stormy waters? Will we learn to work together, each doing her/his part to save the ship and all our lives? Or will we simply go below decks, crawl into our bunks and hope it will blow over before the ship sinks, or let it sink and "end it all."

Have we been fair weather sailors? As long as favorable breezes carry our ship along, we feel we really have little need for each other. It's when the storm comes and the strengths and skills of each person is needed to keep the ship from tearing itself apart in the tumultuous seas and hurricane winds of adversity that we turn to each other. But by then it may be too late. We don't know what the other can do to help save the ship. We have not tried out our skills and our teamwork in the good times given us.

Today, we are probably going through the same kind of storm that occurred about a thousand years before Christ, when the ship was rent asunder and half of the crew—women—were lost. Do we have to lose the whole crew in this, our present storm? Must the survivors be either one or the other? This time, the storm may become so violent the ship will go down and most of us will drown or be cast up on separate islands to lonely out our lives. But we don't have to lose the ship. By our combined skills and strengths, we can get through the storm and sail into bright new worlds never before explored by the human race, worlds in which each person counts, is valued for what that person can contribute to the whole, regardless of gender, but not at the expense of losing one's identity as a woman or as a man.

As "an old man of the sea," one who began sailing at 9 and was building sailboats at 14, graduating to a 16-footer, then to become the owner of a 50-foot yacht, finally crewing on a Caribbean three-masted clipper ship, I can say that learning to sail begins "small." In a 10- or 12-footer, you learn the feel of the wind and the waves and how to respond in a fair breeze, and how to change tactics when the weather kicks up. Moving to a larger craft, the same conditions apply, but now you are thinking and moving in concert with others, perhaps a crew of a half dozen or more. It took 12 of us just to raise the mainsail on the clipper in fair weather and six extra hands to handle running rigging in a blow. Now it is not only what *you* do, but how you coordinate your thoughts and actions with others, at times depending on each other for your very lives!

We embark on "the sea of matrimony," or the adventure of friendship, or of living together prepared for only fair weather, and unwilling to practice the sail-handling and other drills to learn just what each of us is capable of doing, what it is that each brings to the crew to keep the ship sailing not only in fair weather, but when things get tough.

Perhaps if we were not so afraid to fight the little battles, the bigger battles would never occur, or if they did, we'd know more of what to expect of each other. We'd weather the storm, stay in there and pitch, instead of going below decks, avoiding each other and hoping the storm will blow over. Moreover, as you learn to sail the intimate crafts of friendship, of being sweethearts or in marriage, you are preparing yourself for crewing on the larger crafts of the workplace, the club, the action group or in politics. And the experience you get "out there" cooperating to sail "the ship of state" will feed back your skills and attitudes to enrich the running of your more intimate craft. Why can't women and men discuss and problem-solve the running of the craft instead of the running of each other?

Goddess Characteristics in Both Women and Men

The characteristics of the Seven Goddesses in women not only find complementary or counterpart elements in the thinking and feeling of men, but are often identical. They are simply expressed in different ways. For example, the "nest-building" instinct, commonly attributed to birds, bears and other animals, and usually attributed to women, is there in men, too. Traditionally, women have most often expressed their nest-building instincts in furnishing a house, making the interior warm and cozy with "little feminine touches." But what is creating the house, timber by timber, but the same nest-building instinct! And of course, today, women are often found swinging the hammer and saw, while some of the most famous interior decorators are men. Both are exhibiting the same characteristics, even though experiencing role reversal! All in the same boat.

30. Hardware? Software?

Humans are much like computers—or is it the other way around!

Are we gods, trying to make computers into our own image (robots, anyone!)?

Part of what the computer does comes from built-in circuits. In computerese, we say it is "hardwired." This hardwired component performs certain functions and is permanently built into the machine. It's hardware.

Other parts of the computer's behavior and capabilities come from "software." Software programs are "imprinted" on floppy disks or CD ROMs. There are literally thousands of these software programs, available on disks, which can be inserted into the computer to change what it will do, to literally change the way a computer "thinks."

So it is with humans. Our physical being, including our neuronic structure, which determines our unique basic behavior patterns, the *temperament* of each of us, if you will, is hardwired, built-in, can't change, short of some drastic physical insult to the body such as a blow to the head.

But our software comes from the outside. And it is the thousands of "programs" that are pushed into us as we make our trip through life that determine the way each of us *uses* the "hardwiring, " the temperament, she or he has. Our software comes in from the environment, like someone inserting a floppy disk or a CD-ROM and pushing the buttons it takes to activate it—to activate our feelings and our behaviors. So, much of our behavior, what others see us do, is influenced by the various buttons and combinations of buttons that get pushed. So, while your temperament, the basic you, is hardwired, the way you use it, and allow it to be used, is "what comes out here."

And your feelings? What you feel when you respond—either from basic hardwired temperament, or the software that comes at you from the environment, is strictly up to you. You can feel good or bad about what you do, feel drawn toward repeating things that make you feel good, and away from things that make you feel bad. Distinguish between what satisfies your basic temperament, and the feelings that come from a program button-pushed by others, to help you feel out the most satisfying direction in which to turn.

31. Everybody Should Have One

One what? An UNDO button. My Annabelle (my delightful computer) has one. She is the most forgiving creature I've known. Just when I've begun to put my plan into action, I discover a fatal flaw. It won't work. I've messed up. And now I might blow the whole thing. How do I back out of this one? What do I do now?

Almost any ordinary human might simply sit there and laugh. "Serves you right. Think you're so damned smart!"

Not Annabelle. When my thinking has gotten me into an inconceivable snarl, she simply says "Just press my UNDO button. All is forgiven. You can start over."

Can you imagine such understanding, such charity of heart, such an outflowing of that scarce commodity—forgiveness! But that's my Annabelle—that's my new computer. She's hardwired for it. Her "it's-OK-to-make-mistakes" generosity of spirit was built in at the factory. Whichever of her formidable array of buttons I may have pushed wrong in setting up a complicated page, and even forgotten where I started, she wipes out my whole bunch of mistakes with a push of her UNDO button.

If it's so easy to build such forgiveness into a machine, couldn't we begin to implant UNDO buttons in humans?

Looking ahead a little, we could simply breed them in. Perhaps, the first of the characteristics needed by the new

Eves and the new Adams is the acquisition, by any means, of an UNDO button. And, as a man writing this book, I say, "Let the ladies go first, let the Goddesses—all seven of them—have the first go at this UNDO button thing." It might go something like this:

"Mary, did you really mean you think the idea for my next book is lousy?"

"Well, of course not, darling. I've been thinking about it and it has real possibilities. Just push my UNDO button, and I'll press yours." SO I did. And she did. Then we burst out laughing as we went into a big bear hug—instead of a sulk. See what I mean? If the Goddesses would offer us an UNDO button, most of us fellows would not be far behind. We might even beat them to it sometimes!

*Trouble is a part of your life,
and if you don't share it,
you don't give the person who loves you
enough chance to love you enough.*

–Dinah Shore, b. 1917
American entertainer

32. Don't Sweat The Small Stuff

Instead of your "close-up"

—try your wide-angle lens

Too close to the forest to see the trees?

It's an old saying, but each of us—women and men often look through our close-up lens and miss "the big picture" of the whole person. Or of what's going on in a relationship, a job or other life scenario. So when things seem a bit muddled, back off and take a look at the whole scene. Ideally, get away; take a breather for a day or so all by yourself. But if you can't literally "get away from it all," simply get an hour off by yourself, put on your wide-angle lens, sit quietly and let scenes and events drift in and out of your consciousness. Now you can see problems more clearly; see the ones you can do something about, and accept those that are simply not worth bothering about. When you've identified a problem worth your attention, you can put on your close-up lens and see what you need to change—in it, or in yourself.

33. A Zebra? Why Not!

Last night,
I dreamed I was a Zebra

My stripes were just like theirs. To fit the curves of our bodies, the stripes made lovely, flowing lines and patterns. My tribe (they were so much more than just a "herd") had about as many males as females.

I felt so comfortable. Everyone seemed to "fit in"—to know where s/he fit into the scheme of things. The males often stayed on the outside of the group, protecting the tribe from attack. Three or four fighting stallions can cut a lion to ribbons with their sharp, flying hooves. Sometimes, they fought each other, but not often. And they never laid a hoof or a bite on us females.

I felt so good about my female tribe members. The hundred or so were about equally divided among the 7 Goddesses and each seemed to know her part in the tribe's well-being. The Artemis zebras were fast runners and sometimes competed with the males in races across the plains. The Athenas seemed to have a special communication with the males in their councils for the welfare of the tribe. Hestias were quiet, but always saw that things went well. Her mere presence often helped settle any disagreements. Hera was constantly preening to attract one or more of the powerful males with whom she especially wanted to mate. Demeter females were the ones most attentive to their colts, especially their daughters. The playful Persephones kept us all amused. We'd often wonder if they'd ever grow up. Myself, being mainly an Aphrodite, especially appreciated other females with my characteristics, but I sought out the company of the stallions.

Sometimes we'd graze quietly together, then go splashing into some stream, tossing and rolling together in the current. It was sometimes dangerous, but we had more fun than anybody! We had many ways of expressing our sexuality between mating seasons.

What I remember most about my dream was the way each one gave what they had to give, and received graciously what the other had to give. We respected each other; we accepted. When I "come back," I want to be a Zebra.

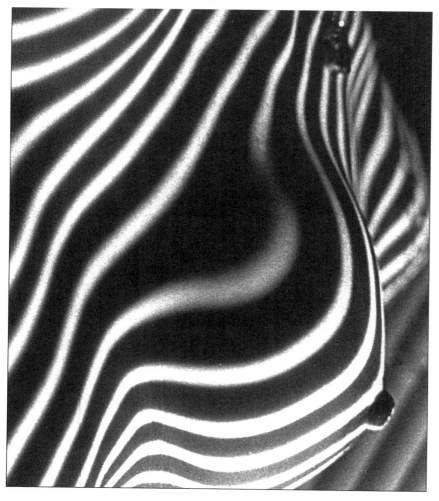

Perhaps the greatest understanding of ourselves (or lack of it!) comes when a person of one sex relates to a person of the opposite sex. *How do **you** relate to a man?* How do you want a man to relate to *you?* How do you really *want* to relate to a man?

Is this the way you relate to a man?

father figure?
friend?
protector?
partner?
co-creator?
lover?
other? ——————

——————

——————

——————

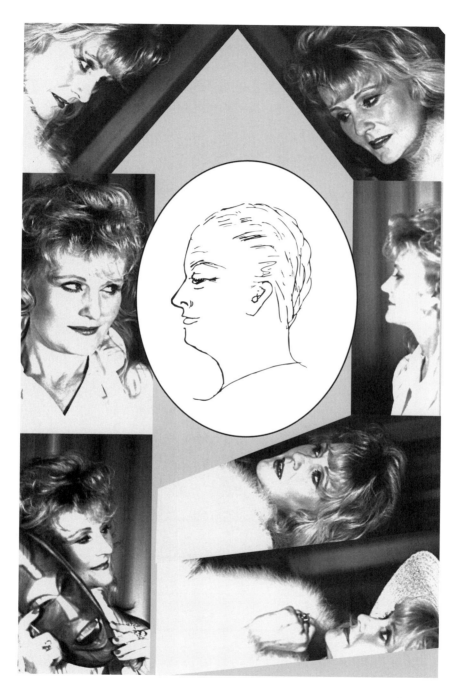

There are so many ways to "love." How do you *really* want to love a man? How do you *like* him? How do you want a man to love you? Will the way *you* love help you in "getting there with Goddess power?"

Is this the way you "love" a man?

clinging?
enveloping?
clawing at his soul?
worshipping him?
phallic symbol?
status symbol?
other? ————————

————————

————————

————————

34. So What Is Love?

"–and on the other hand, Emmy, if he really loved you . . ."

Two Views:

In his book, *The Psychology of Love* (J. P. Tarcher, 1980), Nathaniel Brandon feels confident that "Romantic love is not a myth waiting to be discarded, but, for most of us, a discovery waiting to be born." He points out that "...romantic love becomes the pathway not only to sexual and emotional happiness but also to the higher reaches of human growth."

M. Scott Peck differs strongly. In his book, *The Road Less Traveled* (Simon and Schuster, 1988), he states that "...the myth of romantic love is a dreadful lie." "As a psychiatrist," he says, "I weep in my heart almost daily for the ghastly confusion and suffering that this myth fosters."

Perhaps each of these much respected gentlemen tends to oversimplify. By recognizing that there are many "love-styles," you will be in a better position to refine your own definition of love and determine the kind(s) of love that will work best for you.

Six lovestyles . . . and yours?

Eros is the lovestyle characterized by the search for a beloved whose physical presentation of self embodies an image already held in the mind of the lover. In popular language, it is the pursuit of the lover's "physical type"—his or her ideal image of the beautiful.

Ludus, Ovid's term for playful or game love, describes a style which is permissive and pluralistic (a less loaded word than promiscuous). The degree of involvement is carefully controlled, jealousy is eschewed, and the relationships are often multiple and relatively short lived.

Storge is a style based on slowly developing affection and companionship, a gradual disclosure of self, an avoidance of self conscious passion, and an expectation of long term commitment.

Mania is an obsessive, jealous, emotionally intense lovestyle characterized by preoccupation with the beloved and a need for repeated reassurance of being loved.

Agape is altruistic love, given because the lover sees it as his/her duty to love without expectation or reciprocity. It is gentle, caring and guided by reason more than emotion.

Pragma is a style involving conscious consideration of "vital statistics" about a suitable beloved. Education, vocation, religion, age and numerous other demographic characteristics of the potential beloved are taken into account in the search for a compatible match.

"It is liberating to recognize that love occurs in different ways, that there is not one 'true' style. Each manner of loving has its own appeal." So concluded Steven Prasinos and Bennett I. Tittler in their study of 153 unmarried undergraduates at Vanderbilt University in Nashville, Tennessee. Of the sample, 55% were male, 45% female; age range 17 - 24 years.

Which lovestyle, or lovestyle-mix for *your* Goddess Power?

● 5 billion people = 5 billion lovestyles

Journal of Humanistic Psychology, Winter 1984, Vol. 24, No. 1

The Love Style Game: An Invitation to Play!

Read the first Love-style (Eros) described below. On the opposite page, make a check mark under the name of the Goddess whose Love-style (in your opinion) would most likely match the description. Now read the second Love-style (Ludus) and make a check mark under the Goddess whose characteristics best match that description. Continue down the page, matching each Love-style description with the Goddess you feel is most likely to regard love in the manner described. More than one Love-style may be ascribed to each Goddess.

Eros is the lovestyle characterized by the search for a beloved whose physical presentation of self embodies an image already held in the mind of the lover. In popular language, it is the pursuit of the lover's "physical type" is or her ideal image of the beautiful.

Ludus, Ovid's term for playful or game love, describes a style which is permissive and pluralistic (a less loaded word than promiscuous). The degree of involvement is carefully controlled, jealousy is eschewed and the relationships are often multiple and relatively short lived.

Storge is a style based on slowly developing affection and companionship, a gradual disclosure of self, an avoidance of self-conscious passion, and an expectation of long term commitment.

Mania is an obsessive, jealous, emotionally intense lovestyle characterized by preoccupation with the beloved and a need for repeated reassurance of being loved.

Agape is altruistic love, given because the lover sees it as his/her duty to love without expectation or reciprocity. It is gentle, caring and guided by reason more than emotion.

Pragma is a style involving conscious consideration of "vital statistics" about a suitable beloved. Education, vocation, religion, age and numerous other demographic characteristics of the potential beloved are taken into account in the search for a compatible match

	ARTEMIS	ATHENA	HESTIA	HERA	DEMETER	PERSEPHONE	APHRODITE
Eros							
Ludus							
Storge							
Mania							
Agape							
Pragma							

How would a special person in your life describe your Lovestyle(s)?

Love is the only thing that
we can carry with us when we go,
and it makes the end so easy.

Lousia May Alcott

35. If You Have To Go . . .

If, in spite of your best efforts to give and receive love, you have to go, here are some ways the Seven Goddesses have approached the inevitable.

Perhaps, before you were aware of the seven Goddesses within you, you got into a marriage or relationship that isn't working for either of you. The backgrounds of the two of you are simply so far apart. Your temperaments are so different—you are quick, he is slow, or vice versa. You like to save, he likes to "live it up," or the reverse. Whatever your self-image of who you are and where you want to go is going down the drain. So is his, and you toss the blame back and forth until you can't stand the pain any longer. You've made your best effort to see his point of view as to how life should be lived, and find that your visions of a lifetrip are going steadily in different directions. So it's time to go.

The letter that follows might have been written by you. What comes after, the way each Goddess tells why she has to go, may be helpful in sorting out your own specific reasons for wanting to leave, and communicating them to him. They might even provide clues toward a reconciliation you hadn't thought possible. And, shared with him, they might let each of you start talking again. You might discover the higher ground from which to view each other's self-images and points at which your lifetrips might begin to merge back into a side-by-side journey. Worth a try? Only you can know. But what can you lose?

Dear John,
This is going to be a difficult letter to write, but...

I can see us now, standing under the old oak tree in the moonlight. The leaves made funny shadows across your face, and you said those beautiful words, "I love you, Sheri!"

Yes, I remember that wonderful weekend in the country, walking in the meadows, wading in that ice cold brook, and how you picked me up when I fell down —and all those other wonderful things we did!

The cocktail hours, and the dinners and all those wonderful plans. And some of them came true! For one thing, we got married.

But after a while, things began to happen. We began to draw apart. You began going your way. What was I to do? So I began going my way.

Do you remember how we used to talk? We didn't always agree, but we *talked*. I guess we got afraid of each other. I wish I knew why we stopped talking.

I hope you'll understand, John. I wish there were some way to go back where we started, but I guess we've both become different people. How fortunate we didn't have children. Or would that have helped?

So, perhaps, John, you never really knew me

Actually, John, in going back over it all—what we were to each other, and what we weren't—its probably that I don't really need or want a man in my life any more; probably never really did. I tried to tell you how it was with me, and now you know I'm really...

ARTEMIS

We had a good thing going, I thought. But I guess business is just not your thing and success and the good things in life *are* very important to me. I hope you find someone more attuned to your relaxed view of life. You've been good in so many ways, but I am...

ATHENA

I've tried so hard over the years, John. And I guess you have, too. But your need for the active, gregarious life is, after all, so different from my needs. I've felt so much pressure. I need quiet time for inner-centeredness and to grow spiritually. I had so hoped we'd grow together in body-mind-spirit; but instead we have grown apart. You're a good man, John, but I'm simply...

HESTIA

When I promised to become your wife, John, I expected you to be *my* husband. You say I'm jealous. Well, I am. I can't stand it the way other women look at you, and you at them. There must be *one* man in the world who wants to be *my* husband and I'm going to find him. We'll work things out about the children. I know its hard for you to understand ...

HERA

I do appreciate that you are the father of my children, John, but you seem to have little interest in the family. True, you support us but you don't *do things* with us, or help bring up the kids. I wish you could understand how a mother feels about her children, then maybe you'd be a better father. So I'm taking the children away. I'm seeking a lawyer tomorrow about support. We've been over all this before. You can't change, and I'm...

DEMETER

John, we used to have fun together. We'd go places—out to dinner, dancing, to the beach and all those fun things. But you've forgotten how to play. And you keep asking, "When are you going to grow up?" Well, when are you going to "grow down," back like you were when we were in college together? I'm leaving. The lawyer says you have to pay me good alimony. I'm going to have some fun in life. I'm ...

PERSEPHONE

Yes, John, you have worked up a career in accounting that has given us a good living and it's satisfying to you. But now that my career in advertising and public relations is blossoming, you've been more and more irritated—and irritating. I've got to be out there having creative ideas with people. I can't hang around the house. You should be proud of me. And something else. For some time now, you've been saying I'm over-sexed. Well, I'm simply a real live...

APHRODITE

Ah Love! could you and I with Him conspire
To grasp this sorry Scheme of Things entire,
Would not we shatter it to bits—and then
Re-mould it nearer to the Heart's Desire!

Omar Khayám
1048 - 1122 A.D.

36. Breaking Out

"Veil of Life"
This Painting Hangs In My Living Room

Women and men alike are fascinated by its mysterious depths.
Often, standing beside them, I will ask, "What's going on here?"
Sometimes I'd hear things like, "She is no longer afraid to be seen
as a whole person." Or, "I've often wished I could do that!" And
many other things awakened by the drama of experiencing the
unfolding of a person before their very eyes.

> Painting by Raymond A. Whyte, 28 x 38
> *In collection of the author.*

Emerging You.

What Now?

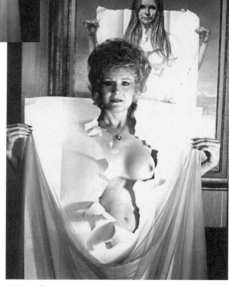

It hurts!

Breaking Out...

*Look!
I'm doing it!*

See...it's me!

It's easier than you think!

Is that all...

I did it.

that was holding me back?

I did it,
so can you.
So can
every
woman.

I feel so GOOD!

When we walk to the edge
    of all the light we have,
And take the step into
    the darkness of the unknown,
We must believe one of two things
    will happen—
There will be something solid
    for us to stand on,

Or we will be taught to fly!

        ...Author unknown

37. A Woman Can Be Anything She Wants To Be

–but she can be some things better than others

There is an old saying: the whole is greater than the sum of its parts. Yet, each part is needed to make up the whole. And as each part of the human body—arms, legs, head, heart, lungs, etc., serves a different function, so each Goddess serves a different function in a woman's total psyche. Thus, Artemis, Athena, Hestia, Hera, Demeter, Persephone and Aphrodite—each one a player in the symphony of a woman's life—in her total body-mind-spirit. As you learn to let each Goddess "do her thing" in her time, you will touch similar harmonies in other women and in men. You will have learned what you want, and how to get it.

Artemis

A Woman Can Be Anything She Wants To Be ❂ 191

Athena

A Woman Can Be Anything She Wants To Be ☯ 193

Hestia

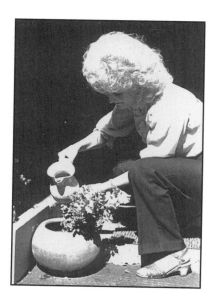

Hera

A Woman Can Be Anything She Wants To Be 🌀 197

Demeter

A Woman Can Be Anything She Wants To Be ☯ 199

Persephone

Aphrodite

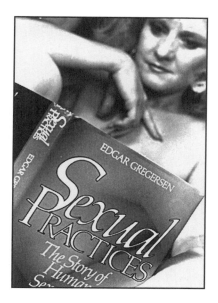

Which Goddess would be most comfortable in this scenario?

Put a "1" in front of the Goddess you feel would be the *most* comfortable in this scenario, a "2" in front of the next most comfortable, and so on. Your "7" will indicate the Goddess *least* comfortable in these situations.

___ Artemis
___ Athena
___ Hestia
___ Hera
___ Demeter
___ Persephone
___ Aphrodite

I would like to be in this scenario (check-mark your choice on the line below)

Not at all		A little			Quite a bit				I'd love it!	
0	1	2	3	4	5	6	7	8	9	10

Whether or not I'd LIKE to be here, if it were necessary for me to do it, I would have to develop more of *the following* Goddess characteristics: (Refer back to Goddess Characteristic Chart on Page 21 and make your list) ....

_____

_____

_____

_____

_____

_____

_____

_____

_____

A Woman Can Be Anything She Wants To Be ⚇ 205

Which Goddess would be most comfortable in this scenario?

Put a "1" in front of the Goddess you feel would be the *most* comfortable in this scenario, a "2" in front of the next most comfortable, and so on. Your "7" will indicate the Goddess *least* comfortable in these situations.

___Artemis
___Athena
___Hestia
___Hera
___Demeter
___Persephone
___Aphrodite

I would like to be in this scenario (check-mark your choice on the line below)

Not at all			A little			Quite a bit			I'd love it!	
0	1	2	3	4	5	6	7	8	9	10

Whether or not I'd LIKE to be here, if it were necessary for me to do it, I would have to develop more of *these* Goddess characteristics. (Refer back to Goddess Characteristic Chart on Page 21 and make your list) ....

Photo courtesy *Del Monte Aviation*, Monterey Peninsula Airport, Monterey, California.

GODDESS GAME THIRTEEN

Which Goddess would be most comfortable in this scenario?

Put a "1" in front of the Goddess you feel would be the *most* comfortable in this scenario, a "2" in front of the next most comfortable, and so on. Your "7" will indicate the Goddess *least* comfortable in these situations.

___Artemis
___Athena
___Hestia
___Hera
___Demeter
___Persephone
___Aphrodite

I would like to be in this scenario (check-mark your choice on the line below)

Not at all			A little			Quite a bit			I'd love it!	
0	1	2	3	4	5	6	7	8	9	10

Whether or not I'd LIKE to be here, if it were necessary for me to do it, I would have to develop more of *these* Goddess characteristics. (Refer back to Goddess Characteristic Chart on Page 21 and make your list) ....

_____
_____
_____
_____
_____
_____
_____
_____
_____
_____

Which Goddess would be most comfortable in this scenario?

Put a "1" in front of the Goddess you feel would be the *most* comfortable in this scenario, a "2" in front of the next most comfortable, and so on. Your "7" will indicate the Goddess *least* comfortable in these situations.

___Artemis
___Athena
___Hestia
___Hera
___Demeter
___Persephone
___Aphrodite

I would like to be in this scenario (check-mark your choice on the line below)

Not at all		A little		Quite a bit			I'd love it!	
0	1	2	3	4	5	6	7	8	9	10

Whether or not I'd LIKE to be here, if it were necessary for me to do it, I would have to develop more of *these* Goddess characteristics. (Refer back to Goddess Characteristic Chart on Page 21 and make your list) ....

_____
_____
_____
_____
_____
_____
_____
_____

Photo courtesy *The Sardine Factory*, Monterey, California.

A Woman Can Be Anything She Wants To Be ⬤ 211

Which Goddess would be most comfortable in this scenario?

Put a "1" in front of the Goddess you feel would be the *most* comfortable in this scenario, a "2" in front of the next most comfortable, and so on. Your "7" will indicate the Goddess *least* comfortable in these situations.

___Artemis
___Athena
___Hestia
___Hera
___Demeter
___Persephone
___Aphrodite

I would like to be in this scenario (check-mark your choice on the line below)

Not at all		A little			Quite a bit				I'd love it!	
0	1	2	3	4	5	6	7	8	9	10

Whether or not I'd LIKE to be here, if it were necessary for me to do it, I would have to develop more of *these* Goddess characteristics. (Refer back to Goddess Characteristic Chart on Page 21 and make your list) ....

_____
_____
_____
_____
_____
_____
_____
_____

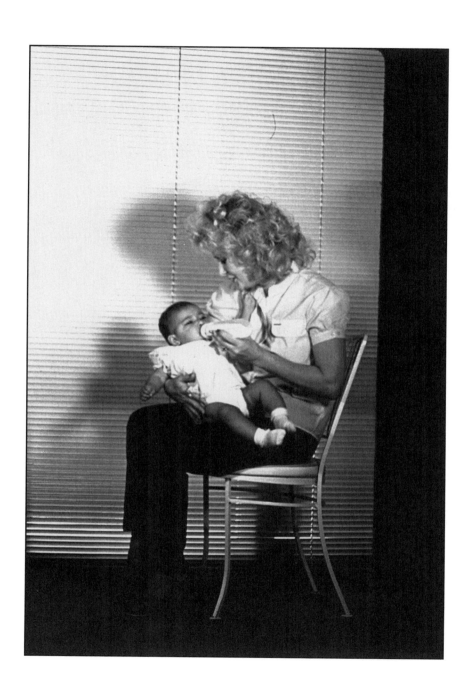

A Woman Can Be Anything She Wants To Be ◯ 213

Which Goddess would be most comfortable in this scenario?

Put a "1" in front of the Goddess you feel would be the *most* comfortable in this scenario, a "2" in front of the next most comfortable, and so on. Your "7" will indicate the Goddess *least* comfortable in these situations.

___Artemis
___Athena
___Hestia
___Hera
___Demeter
___Persephone
___Aphrodite

I would like to be in this scenario (check-mark your choice on the line below)

Not at all			A little			Quite a bit			I'd love it!	
0	1	2	3	4	5	6	7	8	9	10

Whether or not I'd LIKE to be here, if it were necessary for me to do it, I would have to develop more of *these* Goddess characteristics. (Refer back to Goddess Characteristic Chart on Page 21 and make your list) ....

_____

_____

_____

_____

_____

_____

_____

_____

A Woman Can Be Anything She Wants To Be 215

Which Goddess would be most comfortable in this scenario?

Put a "1" in front of the Goddess you feel
would be the *most* comfortable in this
scenario, a "2" in front of the next most
comfortable, and so on. Your "7" will
indicate the Goddess *least* comfortable in
these situations.

___Artemis
___Athena
___Hestia
___Hera
___Demeter
___Persephone
___Aphrodite

I would like to be in this scenario (check-mark your choice on
the line below)

Not at all			A little			Quite a bit			I'd love it!	
0	1	2	3	4	5	6	7	8	9	10

Whether or not I'd LIKE to be here, if it were necessary for
me to do it, I would have to develop more of *these* Goddess
characteristics. (Refer back to Goddess Characteristic Chart
on Page 21 and make your list) ....

_____
_____
_____
_____
_____
_____
_____
_____
_____

A Woman Can Be Anything She Wants To Be 🌓 217

38. Reaching For Your
Higher Consciousness

Your Goddess Consciousness is more than an awareness of a set of attributes that make up your personality. Deep within you, and within all of us, is a yearning to move to a higher level of body-mind-spirit conscious awareness. Let's explore.

What is the center of your consciousness, that within you which occupies your thoughts and directs your energies toward what you want? Quite naturally, as a simple member of the animal kingdom, your first concerns are for food and shelter. Once you've gotten "enough" to satisfy those needs, then what? Now you are free to let your consciousness roam toward finding pleasurable sensations and activities. Enjoying these, you are beginning to feel that if "enough is enough," more is better and your consciousness begins to center on power. "How can I get more people to give me what I want?" Some people never get beyond concerns for security, sensation and power. But the real rewards come when you break through to higher levels of consciousness, to new centers of self-realization, your true Goddess Consciousness.

Earlier in the book we discussed "multilevel learning." Think about your own "learning curve." It is never the smooth upward sweeping line portrayed in most psychology books. Actually, learning is a multilevel process. Learning proceeds level-by-level.

Each of us has had the experience of working at a skill and feeling we were not learning very well, or not at all. Our learning seems to remain stuck at the same level. Then one day we realize, "I've got it!" Now we feel ready to literally leap to a higher level of learning. What we have already learned makes a platform or "runway" from which we may rise and take off to a new level of learning, much as an airplane gathers lifting power as it speeds down the airfield. Once off the ground, it levels off to gain more flying speed before ascending to higher and higher levels. Now you are flying free and clear and "the sky is the limit."

Beyond the security, sensation and power centers are realms of conscious awareness from which you begin to tap the deeper powers of your subconscious mind. Psychologists and psychiatrists point out that when thoughts are conveyed to your subconscious mind, impressions are made on the brain cells. As soon as your subconscious mind accepts any idea, it proceeds to put it into effect immediately. As you open yourself to higher levels of consciousness, you are learning to see the world with greater acceptance. As the song goes, you begin to "have a smile on my face for the whole human race," and you are beginning to know what it is to really live and to love unconditionally.

As you gain "flying speed" you find yourself ascending to a new level, the "Cornucopia Center," where must-hate addictions give way to *preferences*. Now you begin to feel you have all you really want. Now, the world seems to be opening up to give you even *more* than you need to be happy. From the Cornucopia center you may choose to ascend to even higher levels of consciousness.

In the next two pages you will get an overview of this multilevel trip to higher consciousness. I have been privileged to set my feet on the road, or to "try my wings" upward, toward the higher consciousness centers under the guidance of the venerable Ken Keyes, Jr., author of the book, *The Handbook to Higher Consciousness*. Not only has the book sold over 1,000,000 copies, but it has been the baseline for his workshops usually programmed for a full week and attended by thousands over the past twenty years. They came in groups ranging from a dozen to scores of women and men of all ages.

I shall be forever grateful for attending many of his Living Love Workshops. But I treasure even more our private conversations during which I learned of the many levels he experienced as he ascended toward ever higher levels of conscious awareness. Here was a man who practiced what he preached. He, himself, loves unconditionally, and he is beloved by all who meet him.

The Seven Centers of Consciousness, beginning on the next page, were developed over the years by Ken Keyes as the basis for his Living Love Workshops and his ongoing Training Center. As you read them, beginning with the Security Center at the bottom of the page, sense your Goddess Consciousness ascending, level-by-level. While you (and most of us) may not reach the Seventh Center, we can enjoy the refreshment of spirit as we move upward. As someone has said, "Getting there is half the fun!

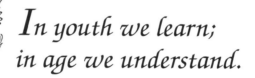

In youth we learn;
in age we understand.

–Marie Ebner-Eschenbach (1830-1916)
Austrian writer

The Seven Centers of Consciousness

A loving person lives in a loving world. A hostile person lives in a hostile world. Everyone you meet is your mirror.

4. THE LOVE CENTER

At this Center you are transcending subject-object relationships and are learning to see the world with the feelings and harmonies of flowing acceptance. You see yourself in everyone—and everyone in yourself. You feel compassion for the suffering of those caught in the dramas of security, sensation, and power. You are beginning to love and accept everyone unconditionally—even yourself.

3. THE POWER CENTER.

When your consciousness is focused on this Center, you are concerned with dominating people and situations and increasing your prestige, wealth, and pride —in addition to thousands of more subtle forms of hierarchy, manipulation, and control.

2. THE SENSATION CENTER.

This Center is concerned with finding happiness in life by providing yourself with more and better pleasurable sensations and activities. For many people, sex is the most appealing of all sensations. Other addictive sensations may include the sound of music, the taste of food, etc.

1. THE SECURITY CENTER.

This Center makes you preoccupied with food, shelter, or whatever you equate with your personal security. This programming forces your consciousness to be dominated by your continuous battle to get "enough" from the world in order to feel secure.

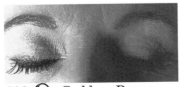

*Love everyone
unconditionally,
including
yourself*

7. THE COSMIC CONSCIOUSNESS
CENTER. When you live fully in the Seventh
Center of Consciousness, you are ready to
transcend self-awareness and become pure
awareness. At this ultimate level, you are one with
everything —you are love, peace, energy, beauty,
wisdom, clarity, effectiveness, and oneness.

6. THE CONSCIOUS-AWARENESS CENTER.
It is liberating to have a Center from which your
Conscious-awareness watches your body and mind perform
on the lower five centers. This is a meta-center from which
you non-judgmentally witness the drama of your body and
mind. From this Center of Centers, you learn to impartially
observe your social roles and life games from a place that is
free from fear and vulnerability.

5. THE CORNUCOPIA CENTER.
When your consciousness is illuminated by this Center,
you experience the friendliness of the world you are creating.
You begin to realize that you've always lived in a perfect
world. To the degree that you still have addictions, the
perfection lies in giving you the experience you need to get free
of your emotion-backed demands. As you reprogram your
addictions, the perfection will be experienced as a continuous
enjoyment of the here and now in your life. As you become
more loving and accepting, the world becomes a "horn of
plenty" that gives you more than you need to be happy.

A beautiful aspect of the consciousness
scale is that each time you go up a step in the
scale, your life gives you:

1. **More energy.**
2. **More contact with people.**
3. **More enjoyment.**

from *The Handbook
To Higher Consciousness*
**Seventh Edition
by
Ken Keyes, Jr.**
By Permission.
Over 1,000,000 copies sold.

An important characteristic of the three lower Centers is that you can never get enough to enjoy your life continuously when you are using the security, sensation, and power filters to interpret the here-and-now in your life. You can use these filters to make limited improvements in your life. But out of the billions of people who have lived on earth, no one has experienced *enough* security, *enough* delightful sensations, and *enough* power to be continuously happy and fulfilled. The experience of *enoughness* only starts as you begin to relax and let your consciousness flow more and more from the Fourth Center—the Love Center, moving upward toward your best self.

Happiness
happens
when your
consciousness is
not dominated
by addictions
and demands—and
you experience life
as a Parade of Preferences

And you'll be
Getting There With Goddess Power!

39. The Seasons of Your Life

As you have moved through these pages, you have probably become increasingly aware of an inspiring concept: The seasons of your life. You have come to understand that as you move through the years, some of your Goddesses have become—or will become, naturally more predominant at various times. Earlier years, perhaps, a Persephone time as you adapt to the needs of others to assure your shelter and care. Adolescence and early adulthood may bring out the identity-seeking, independent Artemis. Economic needs and choices often call up Athena qualities. The "essential man" can switch on Hera and marriage. Hestia and homemaking may follow, perhaps blended with Athena and Demeter.

Children raised and out of the nest may bring on a resurgence of Artemis, the enthusiast for strongly felt causes. Athena may send you back-to-school and back-to-work. Or you may decide to give Aphrodite full reign, unleashing your sensuality, sexuality, creativity and sampling a variety of relationships. In later years, Hera may again beckon, and still later, quiet Hestia welcomes you with open arms—or she may have been with you all the way to light up your spiritual life.

As you have claimed your Goddess Power, you have learned to mix and match your goddesses to the occasion. You have also learned to "shift gears" among your Goddesses over periods of time. And you have come to understand the comfort of "going with the flow" of your life-seasons. Becoming increasingly aware of the range of your options, you have felt more in control of your life and the enjoyment of each of your Goddesses—on call, or in their turn, knowing they are there when you need them. The poem that follows may take you back in time—or back to the future—walking hand-in-hand with each of your Goddesses. Enjoy!

...those first sweet, innocent
    juices of life began to flow,
And as I look back,
    I know I held them in my body
As surely as at this moment
    I hold this glass of wine

The Seasons of Your Life

To everything there is a season,
and a time to every purpose
under heaven.
                    —Ecclesiastes

Although as yet
    I had no egg,
The touch of Demeter
    that early spring
Brought the first stirrings
    of motherhood.

I can feel it now,
    my body opening, even as
The buds opening in the garden
    began unfolding within me,
    began the mysterious journey
    of womanhood.

I was six, and even then
    those first sweet, innocent
    juices of life began to flow.
And as I look back,
    I know I held them in my body
As surely as at this moment
    I hold this glass of wine,
Still untouched, yet all too soon,
    to be quaffed

As life rushed headlong
   into the fullness of Spring.
Then mellow summer,
   and richly laden fall,
   toward ultimate winter,
The seasons of our lives.

Doll-mother Demeter
   filled those early years.
   I procreated life into each one,
   nurtured them with names and food,
   first mud cakes,
   then with tiny crusts
My mother showed me how to bake.

But what is that gurgling
   burbling, bubbly feeling
   tapping gently at my shoulder?
It's Persephone! And I am nine.
I play with my kittens,
   I play like a kitten!
I am soft, pliable, I almost always
   do as I am told.

Mid-spring, lush green,
   my body filling out
   in unexpected places.
Where does it all come from?

The little girls down the street,
   the girl next door—
They play With boys.
Who needs boys,
   loud, rough, pushy boys?

Late Spring, thirteen,
  and now my buds begin to open.
My own blossom unfolds, attracts,
  as the garden's honeyed flowers
  bring buzzing bees.
Deep in my subconscious
  I knew, even then
Soon my own blossom would open
  to the gathering of the honey
  and the fertilizing of the egg.

But even as Persephone roamed the fields
  and played with us,
One day, the blood, and
  my mother said,
You now become a woman.

Must I say "goodbye" dear Persephone?
  As though to answer,
Some days she did not come.

Often, as I walked alone,
  a strange fullness rose
  within me, yet an emptiness.
I felt a void needing to be filled.
In my dreams, strange visions of Apollo.

Before my eyes, boys become men.
The fullness and the emptiness
  become more intense, sweet pain.
I re-create myself—I am Aphrodite!
  I am seventeen.

Now the tides of womanhood
    surged up more often.
Although on some days
    I was still a girl,
Relentless magnets seemed to draw me
    toward all male creatures.
As soon as I came
    within their field of energy,
That same energy of attraction
    became a force for repelling.
I wanted, and I feared
    what I wanted.

One night, under the stars,
    I knew—and was known.
Apollo took me,
    and Oh, in that night,
so willingly, so joyfully,
    my Aphrodite honey flowed!

Two dark nights later,
    came Artemis with pointing finger.
"Come join with me," she said,
    "with the male of the specie,
You are better dead!"

I turned to let Artemis
    rush onward through the night.
Days passed, nights passed.
    My soul seemed to shrivel.
Must I be torn apart?
    Must I live without a heart?

Eagerly, in classes taught
    by learned professors,
    I sought answers.
But if they knew,
    they didn't tell;
    they seemed content
    their brains to sell.
And I came twenty-one.

Isn't there some plan of things,
    —a slot where I will fit?
Isn't there something more for me
    than pleasantries and wit?

One day, at dawning,
    in all her glory, stood Athena.
Taking my hand,
    she walked me into a new day.

"Here is useful work to do," she said,
    "side by side with men
And others like yourself."

With growing confidence,
    over days, weeks, months, years,
My feet found new paths.
Rejoicing in my growing self,
    my vision broadened.
I heard myself say such words as
    plan, organize, career.

The wine of life
    coursed in my blood
I wanted it all.

If enough is enough,
More is better!

Then, one day, soft and lovely,
   in the doorway Demeter stood
And mirrored in her eyes
   I saw motherhood.
Hera was, of course, among the goddesses
   of whom I knew, but

I was unprepared for the return
   of that old magnetism: Apollo,
And the re-awakening of Aphrodite in me.
   "It's only natural," said Hera.
   "You are soon to be a wife."

Love, I was to learn, was more
   than the rush of Aphrodite
   through my veins.
Love is what one person
   feels for another
When there is at-one-ment;
   when the happiness of the other
Is essential to the one.

Love, too, I learned, was what
   a mother bird feels
   as she sits on the nest,
   waiting, hoping; then feeding.

Love is the tearing experience of loss
   as the mother must push the fledgling
   off the limb
   to try its wings in the world.

Yes, I schooled myself in the lessons
    of loving others.
But I had failed to learn the lesson
    of loving myself.
Then, out of the quietness of my fatigue
    from restless goings and comings
    in station wagons full of too much energy,
Hestia came and took my hand in hers,
    led me into a stately temple.

There, kneeling with her before the fire
    she so carefully tended, I first beheld
the living flame of love within myself.

The elegance I had learned
    to show the world
Turned to beauty before my eyes.
    I was beautiful, I was lovely,
I loved, for the first time, me.

An empty nest,
    a new regard,
Returned Athena, even a touch of Artemis.
    Now it is I perched on a limb,
Waiting to try my new wings
    in a new world.
I am, indeed, a 20th Century Goddess,
    yes, me—all 7 of me!

True, the years had lessened my energies,
    but I had become friends
    with each of my Goddesses.
To know the Goddesses is to know oneself.
    Now each one stood ready.

As my growing wisdom learned to call them
up,
   each as needed
   to express the different facets
   of emerging me.

It was heady stuff,
   this new freedom to invite
First one Goddess,
then another
   into my body-mind-spirit.

A well met Apollo
A business colleague, my Athena.
The sisterhood of Artemis
   called forth my Aphrodite.

Hestia revived my inner flame
   when needed.
Persephone was always welcome
   when she came to play.
But Hera? Ah-h-so-so-so, perhaps,
   another day.
And now to harvest autumns lovely days,
   to breathe in frosty airs
   to join last dances of red leaves,
to count time in minutes,
   to cherish friends,
   children, grandchildren.

They've known my darkside
   and my lightside,
They have let me hear
   their heartsongs.

They have listened to mine.
Each high, each low we've known
 have added richness to my wine.

Soon enough, first snows
 and flakes to match my hair;
Soon, deep winter, too,
 firesides, memories
 and friends to share.

Gone now, a half century and more,
 I see my glass, my life,

Not half empty, but half full!

I see new colors in the sunset.
I am invited to my transformation
 in tomorrow's morning.
I accept.

The Seasons of Our Lives—How The Poem Came To Be

Immediately on arising on the morning of June 30, 1986, I was propelled to the library to reach into my desk for a sheet of paper. Now, the kitchen table beckoned. There was no time to get down to my office and writing desk. It was 6:37 AM and the first rays of the summer sun had begun to flood the Pacific Ocean but I barely noticed, so eager was my pen for paper. Actually, the poem had begun within me as I lay in bed at the first light of day. Words flowed, then stopped. It was no use. The flow was gone. I forced. Nothing but meaningless, unrelated drivel. My muse had retired for the day.

The following morning at 6:30 the same thing happened. Again I had tapped my stream of consciousness.

Now, the words came faster than my pen would move; but I could read the scratching and that's all that counted in that madness to capture the flow before it might rush past, leaving me again with that hollow, washed out feeling. Then, suddenly, indeed, it stopped. No more words would come. Yet I knew the poem was not finished. But there was nothing to do but put pen and paper away—and wait.

Three weeks later, in the dawn of July 25, my muse again sent me scurrying for paper and my place at the kitchen table, my pen fairly dripping with words to find life on the page. Again, the poem flowed from my depths. It all came so easily and so "right" that later, looking back at my handwriting on the yellow-lined page, there was hardly a faltering or a correction. This time, when the flow stopped, I knew the work was finished. I had been able to move through the life of a woman as she stood in the sunset contemplating the seasons of her being.

How long the poem lay gestating in my subconscious I will never know. But approximately a year earlier I had taken a series of photographs of this same woman, the model you see gracing these pages. Now, here she was, standing on my deck, silhouetted against the ocean aglow with the setting sun, contemplating her life as she sipped wine from a long stemmed glass. Busy with my camera, there were no words then, but I knew one day they would come. For two years, I had read and browsed dozens of books and magazine articles for women, about women and by women. I began, I believe, almost to think like a woman.

A remark by Mary Scott, the night before my first sunrise rendezvous with my muse, may have been the trigger. Mary had come down from Berkeley to spend a couple of days with my wife, Fritzi, and me to go over the manuscript of my book-in-work, *Love Your Seven Goddesses* (since retitled *Goddess Power*). After a somewhat tense day of arguing editorial details, we were relaxing over a glass of wine and browsing through an album of brilliantly colored sunset photographs I had taken over many years.

Philosophically, Mary remarked, "Each sunset is the promise of another day." "Yes," I said, "and of another month and another year and another season in our lives." We were quiet for a moment, then I said, "You know, Mary, I think I could write something about the seasons of our lives for the book. "A poem, perhaps?" asked Mary.

The next morning, it happened.

Looking back, I realize that I had been blessed with the total release of my *anima* (C. G. Jung's concept of the feminine which resides in the psyche of man as well as in woman) to share a transpersonal understanding with the whole wonderful world of womankind.

When One Door Closes

When one door of happiness closes,
   another opens.
But often we look so long
   at the closed door
   that we do not see the one
      which has been opened for us

Helen Keller

40. Why Am I In This Book?

"I guess you've been wondering why I'm in this book?"

I accepted the invitation to model for this book because I would like to help all my sisters (and brothers, too!) by letting them know the wide range of feelings a woman can have, and the many roles she often must play or better yet, to open up options she never thought of or dreamed possible. I want my audience to realize that they are not alone in their feelings of anger, hate, grief, love, sex, joy and reverence—and that often these feelings strike at the most unexpected—and sometimes unwelcome moments, and it's OK.

Being in this book is like being in a play. In it, I have played many roles. Actually, I'm more like an impersonator; partly myself in another woman's shoes to look, think and act as she would.

This is not a book about me. It is a book about Everywoman—about you. For each of us is a part of the sisterhood of women.

It is also a book for every man, for does not every man seek to understand the vagaries, the mystery of woman? Perhaps in pursuing this understanding about the other half, the brotherhood of man will come close to reality, and man will not need to fight wars.

My Dad has told me that he used to try so hard to be "consistent," always responding the same way in the name of "reliability." And he used to wonder why everybody always seemed to be having such a good time—all but himself. "Finally," he said, "one day I just said, 'to hell with it. I'm going to be me'." And from that moment he told me not only did he enjoy life more, he started a new career. And I'm sure that his new work as a writer-educator made him begin to really enjoy life, enabling him to make more of a contribution to society than his years as an up-the-ladder organization man.

I actually remember when he changed. Mom and I and my 9-year-old brother worried "What's to become of us now?"

But Mom had faith in his ideas, and we began finding him so much more of a fun person to live with, we felt doing without a few material things was small discomfort for having a whole new Dad, in person—a real live man, expressing himself in wonderful new ways. We all pitched in. We became a happier family, I can tell you.

And that's how I've come to feel about it—enjoy all these wonderful Goddesses within me! I could be Artemis, Goddess of Nature. Or Athena, Goddess of Wisdom and Crafts. I could be Hestia, Goddess of Hearth and Temple. And there's Hera, Goddess of Marriage. Why not Demeter, Goddess of Grain and Nurture? Or Persephone, Goddess Kore, Eternal Maiden? And I'd certainly consider being Aphrodite, Goddess of Love and Beauty!

But the truth is, I carry some of each of these Goddesses within me. And so does every woman. Best of all, each of us can mix-match them any way we wish to meet a special occasion or situation in our lives. In this book, you have explored ways of getting acquainted with each one of them and using their powers in your everyday life and the work-a-day world. You have gotten a feel for the one(s) you want to strengthen, and for others you may wish to soften up a bit. You have, in a word, been opening up to more options than you ever dreamed possible. You've been finding your Goddess Power. Now do you see why I really wanted to model for this book?

WOMAN,

her
thoughts
reactions
feelings

41. For Sharing

MAN,

his
thoughts
reactions
feelings

Higamus, hogamus

woman is monogamous,

Hogamus, higamus

man is polygamous,

–and Woman now?

And we think we are so far out!

In early times, it was reversed. Women were polygamous. They took men into the temple as and when they wanted to experience sex. It was a part of the Goddess religion. They were not "naturally" monogamous, nor did they behave that way.

That's news to me!

I wonder how women today would feel about this?

Women were forced to become monogamous by men who needed to make sure that they, and not some other man, were the father of a particular child. Now it is reversing again and the old saw is reading "hogamus, higamus, woman is polygamous."

We did that?

Hey, that's great! — or is it?

From earliest civilization, perhaps 30,000 years ago, right up until about a thousand years before Christ, woman ruled. While the men were out hunting, women invented agriculture. By their hard work, they brought forth food from the land. The hunting-gathering way of obtaining food gave way to staying in one place, growing things to eat, domesticating animals and building shelters, then villages and towns. Because women worked the land, they owned it. Women did not care who was the father of her children, as long as she had children—girl children like herself, to whom to pass on her possessions and her land. It was a natural set-up for rule by matriarchy.

So that's how it got started!

Things must have been better then.

The history books didn't tell us about that!

Then came men's power take-over, "The one way we can succeed," they told each other, is by making sure that "this is *my* son, so I can pass my goods and property on to him." Get the property and pass it along to the male child *only* became the order of the day. The reins of civilization changed hands. Now man—patriarchy, was in power.

I never thought of myself as a sinner. What a guilt-trip they laid on us!

Male rule has become increasingly constricting of women's rights over the past several thousand years. The trend was locked in by the Bible story that labeled Eve in the Garden of Eden as the first sinner, making Adam likewise a sinner by tempting him with the forbidden apple. This gave men the perfect reason for closing down the Goddess temples throughout the land, thus depriving women of their last vestige of power. But now, it's all changing again. Women are now telling each other, "We will take back our sexuality!" And power.

It's about time women got a break.

Men have had it their way so long.

Now what will happen to men? —to me?

SEX POWER: "I Never Thought I'd Buy A Condom"

Can't say I think women really want to do this but strongly sexed women won't give up sex, and they don't want babies, or diseases. Or is it...

These words headlined full-page advertisements in four of the nation's most prominent women's national magazines in the Fall of 1986, reaching millions of readers of all ages, from girls in their teens to women of adult maturity. A full-page in another national women's magazine touted the purchase of condoms by women

I could hardly believe my eyes!

What a power trip. Why don't they do like they've always done?

with the headline, "Real sexual equality." Still, a sixth full-page ad encouraging a woman to supply men with the means of safely satisfying her sexual needs, headlines, "Very often the best contraceptive for a woman is the one for a man."

So what do I do now?

"How to Stay Sexual When You Don't Have a Man" by Kiki Olson in November, 1986, Cosmopolitan gives "how to" advice and encouragement. For example, she writes:

I can understand this. It's getting OK for a woman to express her normal and natural feelings toward men. Too long, a man has made us feel it's wrong for us to express our sensuality unless it was only for him.

"Staying sexy...means smiling back at the gorgeous construction worker you pass on your way to the office; touching the hand of the sultry bartender when you pay the tab; waving at the toothsome truck driver who's stopped at a red light....I enjoy the company and attention of men, and I'm able to return that attention—easily." She ends her discourse with, "...as long as you continue to interact and allow yourself the sensual pleasures you can give yourself, you'll be a sexy, vital, exciting woman, feasting on the banquet of life

Here these women are going for just any man, and I don't find it all that easy to attract a woman to me.

that you've created for yourself."

I think it would be good for both of us if men read women's magazines once in a while.

It may be unfortunate that the foregoing advertising and women's writing appeared in media seldom touched by men: women's magazines. Do men know how women really feel when they talk among themselves about "men?" The popular non-gender media too often presents simply a muddle of confusion for both sexes.

Maybe I'd better pick up a woman's magazine and see what's going on with women these days. I thought I knew.

Mixed Messages

Just because a woman wants to stand up for her rights in a still male - dominated society doesn't mean she is giving up her sexuality and the need to have a good self-image and to look like a desirable woman to a man, I don't see the conflict.

Men are getting mixed messages. "I see, on the one hand," my friend, Jim, was telling me, "magazine pages filled with luscious lips, come-on hips and eyes that eat you alive—eyes that say, "Come on to bed—now." His brow furrowed and his head turned from side to side as he continued. "On the other hand," I read newspaper columns and magazine articles about NOW, the National Organization for Women and their militant stand against men across the board. And when I have custody of my two teenage

I can certainly understand Jim's feelings. Such a conflict of messages women are giving men these days!

daughters on weekends, I too often hear, "Hey, Dad, that's sexist!"

I assured him I was quite familiar with the literature and with "sexist" epithets pointed in my direction, often leaving me mystified as to what I'd done to deserve them. I urged him to continue, enjoying his company over a drink at our favorite watering hole.

It's not hard to recall Cleopatra, the Empress Josephine and a few other powerful, sexy women who certainly got their way.

"Intelligent women," he said, thoughtfully, "have always used their sex power to get what they've wanted. And, by and large, down through the ages, we men have loved it—lapped it up."

"So what's happening now, as you see it?"

It's about time!

"What's happening now is that women seem to be coming on with a two-edged sword. In addition to their age-old sex power, they have added a new cutting edge: economic power. Now they seem to want to control by both sex and money."

"You don't believe in equal pay for equal work?" I

challenged.

"I have no quarrel with equal pay for equal work. But it seems to me that, having gotten a taste of power from the women's movement—even though they may not actively participate, women in general now seem to have a thirst for power. I saw a magazine ad the other day in which a woman was pulling a man along by his necktie, like a dog on a leash. She *was* pulling him toward her, but I like to approach a woman in my own way, not literally pulled in by her." Divorced for five years, my friend was considerably in touch with the times and with his own feelings about women and their new attitudes.

Sometimes I wonder. Have we come along a little too far and too fast?

I saw that, too. Of course, the tie pulling was all in fun, but I wonder what I'd say and do if a woman did that to me?

I heard Jim out, this old friend of mine, now in his mid-50's, whom I had not seen for some time. I could have replied, "How lucky can we get—women really wanting us now!" Instead, I looked at his beautifully tailored suit, proper necktie, perfectly folded pocket handkerchief and reminded

Yes, there are too many men out there killing themselves chasing a buck, and forgetting how to be human for themselves, and for a woman.

Could this be me?

myself that, in the dizzying milieu of corporate life in which he traveled, he has scarcely had time to concern himself with the fundamentals of today's reality in man-woman relationships: how we got where we are.

Jim's feelings were honest. They were thrust upon him by the dual tidal waves of our times: the sexual revolution and the women's movement.

Yes, I know women like that. And I have almost been there myself. It's frightening!

The sexual revolution, instead of the "togetherness" it was supposed to bring, actually left many lonely fragments wandering in the outer space of human relationships. Too many of these forlorn fragments were displaced homemakers. And younger women coming up saw traditional man-woman relationships melt before their eyes. Now, too many women were out there fending for themselves, making do on one-earner pay— unequal with men, and with fewer and fewer prospects of marriage and the traditional security of home and family. Men still had their jobs. And for men, there was an increasing field of available women in which to play. Now, more than ever, women were at the mercy of men.

I've been so busy between marriages, I guess I never thought of that.

From this low ebb in the fortunes of womankind, the women's movement was born. A new sisterhood arose. Banding together, women began to fight back. The movement began with a barely noticeable sea change. At first, merely a swell. Then, in the marketplace, in the home and among women and men generally, the seas became choppy. Now there was no doubt that a storm was brewing. It became heavy going. People began to run for cover, women in one direction, men in another. But the tidal wave came on. Now, instead of seeking comfort in each other—in a common lifeboat, they sought only to save themselves.

I lost more than one boy friend in the storm.

I got so I couldn't understand what women wanted.

Then came recognition of woman as a person. A woman could have a credit rating, own property, run for political office, assume management in business and other equal rights opportunities. While ERA and other women's goals have not yet manifested, perhaps the storm is subsiding so that women and men can deal with each other as persons, with gender difference as something to be treasured instead of defining a battleground.

I guess the storm's not completely over. Things are getting better, but we've still got a lot of problems.

Thank God, things are getting better.

Backlash or Appreciation?

My friend, I reflected, was echoing the feelings of many— some say perhaps a half of all American men today, who are now being touched in new ways by women in two major areas of their lives, jobs and sex: women's competition in the marketplace and women's sexual take-over. They are experiencing feelings of backlash. They are being attacked on two fronts in territory that has for centuries been their turf.

It's not sexual "take-over." It's just needing to feel we can be free to express our sensuality. and, at times, our full Aphrodite sexuality.

It's tough, especially for the younger men coming up. They sometimes wonder, "What's wrong with me?"

But men with these feelings have a choice. In the marketplace, they can wallow in the negative feelings of backlash, letting their "underdog" feelings

Women's natural nurturing qualities could counter men's seemingly destructive nature, behavior that leads to heart attack in the workplace and to war in the world. Women don't want their babies to grow up and get killed in wars. Men don't seem to mind.

damage their careers, or they can welcome a new warm and nurturing touch in the conduct of everyday business, a touch unique to the psychobiological qualities of womankind. The "feminine mystique" could bring new perspective into the work environment, birthing new ideas for improved working conditions and perhaps more profit for both employees and management. And a better chance for peace on earth.

In the sex scenario, men can fight their feelings of powerlessness by striking back with violence against women or by retreating into homosexuality or some other male-only world. Or they can accept their good fortune and *go with* woman's newly expressed sexual needs.

Economic and sexual considerations are equally important and each needs exploring as a woman and a man begin to entwine their lives. However, here I'd like to share my knowledge of one choice a

Actually, the more I think about it, having women around me on the job adds a little more spice. There's a softness, a kindness in the air I didn't feel before. I think other fellows are feeling this, too.

man can make in the sexual realm: Go with it!

Go with it —and let her tell me what to?

What follows may seem addressed to men but, hopefully, both men and women are reading this together now. In any event, I have been told by most of the women who have been kind enough to advise and consult with me in preparing this book that women like to know how men think and feel at their end of their sexual scenario. They'd like to listen in on a conversation, as one man might talk to another, sharing his knowledge of the territory by relating his trip—and giving evidence not only of survival, but the heartwarming beauty of the journey—in spite of the heartaches. I would tell of my transition from backlash to appreciation. I would tell how it has made me a better man. And I would begin addressing my male friend(s) something like this:

I'm glad there's at least one man willing to listen to us.

Men don't open up and tell us how they feel. Will this guy really do that?

This guy could be right on!

Instead of feeling robbed of your sexual power, revel in being more *genuinely wanted* by women. Let a woman lead you.

This man know his biology — and a bit more about women than most men.

She wants to have your masculinity, your male power, your total he-man sexuality, programmed her way. You may not realize it, but biologically, women are more finely tuned sensually and sexually than men. They can teach us a lot. Try it, you'll like it!

Back to school and I love it!

You are not giving up your power as a man, you are making the most of it by using it where it will be most rewarding— rewarding to you, by delighting, exciting and bringing out the most woman in her. And isn't this what you wanted in the first place?

Sure it's what I want.

I can feel my Aphrodite rising to the occasion!

Let her guide your hands, your body, your mind. She wants the best of your manhood, the most of your strength, the most exquisite of all you want to give her. I know; I wish I had known sooner.

I can feel my "expectation" rising!

I went through three stages. First, in my marriage at 21 (I did not have sex before then) I held the sex act as something sacred. My mother had imbued me with the idea and I was actually afraid to feel the pleasure I felt! To enjoy might be evil. Further, I thought I might hurt her and so withheld much of my vigor, robbing both her and myself of perhaps the Creator's greatest gift—the joy of sex. There was a child, for which we were both thankful. But we missed so much. These days it is difficult to believe, but in all our thirteen married years, I never saw my wife in the nude.

Poor woman!

Poor man!

He must have been a prude, but I guess it was like that back then.

The second coming (literally!) began with my second marriage. Divorced, released from World War II Navy duty, and 36, I brought to her a wild passion dammed up inside of me from my early teens. Here, finally, was a woman to take me where I was, in all my innocence, and guide my total male power into the most explosive orgasm a man could dream of, and give me back the total womanness of her body-mind-spirit. For the first time, I was made whole, a total man. After thirteen luscious years, we divorced over what seems now to

She must have been something! But I could do a lot for a man who really appreciated my full-out Aphrodite!

Lucky man! Why can't I find a woman like that?

be trivial issues. Over the years, I have become ever more thankful that I had this woman as my "great teacher" in the arts and techniques of making love.

My third stage came with freedom and position as a writer giving me access to many women. Being fresh from my wonderful years of learning, and now with the confidence born of experience, I suppose I thought I knew it all and I approached women with a typical male power attitude. But soon, I was remembering the earliest years of my second stage and began letting the woman guide me to satisfy her needs. I moved in this direction because it satisfied more of my needs, released more of my powers, passions, delights. And each woman taught me something.

Sexual desire is inborn; the sexual arts and skills are learned. Skill and technique is not the intellectual invasion of the heart it might at first seem to be. Rather, like golf or tennis or sailing a boat, skill and

A Don Juan?

This says it all! Why does it have to take so long for women and men to learn how to have all those wonderful things together?

There may be a lesson here.

I think I've been missing the big picture. To have all this will take time— more time than I've been willing to give. Well, I'm learning. Candlelight, wine—and time .

technique enable you to put more of your whole self into the act and get more emotional electricity flowing into your total being. Now you are becoming less conscious of using skills and techniques and more of an artist, blending them with every atom of your being into enjoying your peak performance, the blast-off into outer space—the realization of what the Goddess Aphrodite can really be!

*(Last night, he made me feel like a **real** woman!)*

Aphrodite made me feel like the real man I want to be. Such power I had...I gave, and what I got!

Most of all, you become a co-creative artist as a partner in the give-and-take of love-making. Every atom of your being comes alive in the dance of life as the two of you share the most complete melding of body-mind-spirit it is the privilege of two human beings to have.

So, my friend(s), let the lady lead. Rejoice in the glories of the Goddess Aphrodite released! You have nothing to lose, but you will gain deepest sexual pleasure and the affirmation of your total manhood.

While this book is obviously

written for women, I hope that you, as a woman reader, have invited your "boy friend," "male companion," "spouse," or "friend" to read the foregoing "For Sharing" pages (even the whole book!). With new mutual understandings, you may find yourselves on a new and higher plateau of common ground on which to share a more equal footing. Together, you just might invent a new Adam and a new Eve—leaving out the apple.

42. Try Them On For Size

*And the trouble is,
if you don't risk anything,
you risk even more.*

-Erica Jong, b. 1942
American writer

On the stage of life, which parts will be the most comfortable, the most exciting, the most like *you* to play?

We've talked about your Goddess-mix, how your special blend of 2 or 3 or 4 probably best defines you, the woman. However, it may be useful to know your "leading lady." She is the one who, standing alone on the stage of your life, would be your major resource of strength and the one who may best represent the real you—the way you are now. Or, she may be the one you'd like to be but feel her stature would be too difficult to attain. To find out, try them on for size. Which one is the best fit. As you look at yourself in the mirror "wearing her", does she look like the *you* you feel like —or would like to be? Perhaps she does. But how will you feel *living* as the Goddess out there in the world for all to see and react to? To find out, wear her for a full day and *be* like you visualize she is in everyday flesh-blood body ALL DAY. How did others react to her? Did their glances, their actions make you feel good? Did they seem to be coming toward you or moving away? Would they like you like this tomorrow—or do they signal, "I wish you weren't like this!"

Now, with the next two pages, "try them on for size!"

TRY THEM ON FOR SIZE!

Cut out all 7 Goddess cards below and on the next two pages.

Each day for 7 days*, put one card up on your mirror and, for all that day, *be* that Goddess.

- Dress the way she would dress
- Speak the way she would speak
- Walk the way she would walk
- Eat the way she would eat
- Act toward others the way she would act
- Think about others the way she would think about her co-workers, her boss, other women and men in her life.

LIVE THAT GODDESS ALL DAY!

At the end of the day take the card down, turn it over, and on the back, and with your pencil in hand, express your feelings, how it really felt–your exploring, your discovering, your learning during that day.

*Note: You may wish to spend your day with each Goddess over a period of time, say one day each week for 7 weeks. But don't miss the chance to *live* them.

- - - - - - - CUT ALONG DOTTED LINE - - - - - - -

The Goddess Artemis

feels equal to men	
affiliate of women	
strong sense of identity	
activist	
strongly felt causes	
nature lover	
assertive	
independent	
athletic	
men not needed	

- - - - - - - CUT ALONG DOTTED LINE - - - - - - -

ARTEMIS

In my role as Artemis, most of the day I felt (place mark (√) along the line):

NOT GOOD	FAIRLY GOOD	QUITE GOOD	REALLY GOOD
1	2	3	4

I would like to be more like Artemis:

NEVER	SOMETIMES	ALMOST ALWAYS	ALWAYS
1	2	3	4

The qualities I like most about Artemis are	(√)
feels equal to men	
affiliate of women	
strong sense of identity	
activist	
strongly felt causes	
nature lover	
assertive	
independent	
athletic	
men not needed	

The Goddess Athena

men as colleagues	
high achiever	
mature strategist	
cool under fire	
priority: own needs	
authoritative	
confident	
interest in world affairs	
physically active	
chaste	

The Goddess Hestia

spiritual	
non-assertive	
no sense of pressure	
quiet, introspective	
domestic	
orderly housekeeper	
inner centeredness	
loves rituals	
"old soul" presence	
excellent counselor	

ATHENA

In my role as Athena, most of the day I felt (place mark (√) along the line):

NOT GOOD	FAIRLY GOOD	QUITE GOOD	REALLY GOOD
1	2	3	4

I would like to be more like Athena:

NEVER	SOMETIMES	ALMOST ALWAYS	ALWAYS
1	2	3	4

The qualities I like most about Athena are	(√)
men as colleagues	
high achiever	
mature strategist	
cool under fire	
priority: own needs	
authoritative	
confident	
interest in world affairs	
physically active	
chaste	

HESTIA

In my role as Hestia, most of the day I felt (place mark (√) along the line):

NOT GOOD	FAIRLY GOOD	QUITE GOOD	REALLY GOOD
1	2	3	4

I would like to be more like Hestia:

NEVER	SOMETIMES	ALMOST ALWAYS	ALWAYS
1	2	3	4

The qualities I like most about Hestia are	(√)
spiritual	
non-assertive	
no sense of pressure	
quiet, introspective	
domestic	
orderly housekeeper	
inner centeredness	
loves rituals	
"old soul" presence	
excellent counselor	

The Goddess Hera

marriage first, career second	
wife first, mother second	
personal friendships, second	
seeks status symbol life	
heroic in support of mate	
blind to mate's defects	
jealous	
watchful	
radiant when happy	
shrew when betrayed	

The Goddess Demeter

loving	
motherhood paramount	
loves pregnancies	
enjoys serving others	
patient, persevering	
generous	
solid, dependable	
volunteering	
not "ambitious"	
"feminine" jobs	

HERA

In my role as Hera, most of the day I felt (place mark (√) along the line):

NOT GOOD	FAIRLY GOOD	QUITE GOOD	REALLY GOOD
1	2	3	4

I would like to be more like Hera:

NEVER	SOMETIMES	ALMOST ALWAYS	ALWAYS
1	2	3	4

The qualities I like most about Hera are	(√)
marriage first, career second	
wife first, mother second	
personal friendships, second	
seeks status symbol life	
heroic in support of mate	
blind to mate's defects	
jealous	
watchful	
radiant when happy	
shrew when betrayed	

DEMETER

In my role as Demeter, most of the day I felt (place mark (√) along the line):

NOT GOOD	FAIRLY GOOD	QUITE GOOD	REALLY GOOD
1	2	3	4

I would like to be more like Demeter:

NEVER	SOMETIMES	ALMOST ALWAYS	ALWAYS
1	2	3	4

The qualities I like most about Demeter are	(√)
loving	
motherhood paramount	
loves pregnancies	
enjoys serving others	
patient, persevering	
generous	
solid, dependable	
volunteering	
not "ambitious"	
"feminine" jobs	

The Goddess Persephone

extremely feminine	
compliant in nature	
can be "sex-kitten"	
adapts to wishes of others	
likes to be sheltered	
lacks direction	
difficulty following through	
rebellious	
manipulative	
dream oriented	

The Goddess Aphrodite

sensual, passionate	
unconventional	
creative, enthusiastic	
need variety in work	
need variety in men	
"here and now" attitude	
art, music, dance, poetry	
lover of laughter	
wide circle of friends	
not possessive, jealous	

PERSEPHONE

In my role as Persephone, most of the day I felt (place mark (√) along the line):

NOT GOOD	FAIRLY GOOD	QUITE GOOD	REALLY GOOD
1	2	3	4

I would like to be more like Persephone:

NEVER	SOMETIMES	ALMOST ALWAYS	ALWAYS
1	2	3	4

The qualities I like most about Persephone are	(√)
extremely feminine	
compliant in nature	
can be "sex-kitten"	
adapts to wishes of others	
likes to be sheltered	
lacks direction	
difficulty following through	
rebellious	
manipulative	
dream oriented	

CUT ALONG DOTTED LINE - - - - - - -

APHRODITE

In my role as Aphrodite, most of the day I felt (place mark (√) along the line):

NOT GOOD	FAIRLY GOOD	QUITE GOOD	REALLY GOOD
1	2	3	4

I would like to be more like Aphrodite:

NEVER	SOMETIMES	ALMOST ALWAYS	ALWAYS
1	2	3	4

The qualities I like most about Aphrodite are	(√)
sensual, passionate	
unconventional	
creative, enthusiastic	
need variety in work	
need variety in men	
"here and now" attitude	
art, music, dance, poetry	
lover of laughter	
wide circle of friends	
not possessive, jealous	

CUT ALONG DOTTED LINE - - - - - - -

43. Has Your Goddess Profile Changed?

You came into this book with one set of ideas about yourself. You looked in your Goddess mirror and put down what you saw. Have your ideas about yourself—the kind of person you really are—changed?

Without looking back at your first Goddess Characteristics Checklist, turn to pages 271 and 272 and check off your Goddess Characteristics and write under the Goddess pictures as you see yourself *now*. Put down what you now see in your Goddess mirror. Then turn back and compare it with the one you did at the beginning of your encounter with the Seven Goddesses—and with yourself—as you have taken them into your life.

Have you a better idea of what you really want in life —and how to get it? Have you begun to feel you can trust your vision of your best self—and what you need to do to move in your chosen direction?

In completing this book, you've had a lot to take in within a relatively short time. Are you aware that the power of your subconscious mind will be at work sorting things out for you as you go about your daily work, home life—and even as you sleep? Are you willing to wait patiently for the moment your subconscious mind walks through the door of your conscious mind to hand you a new idea to act upon—to follow your own wisdom?

If your answer to "all of the above" is affirmative, we

have had a good journey together. Now, the open road is yours! Get there with Goddess Power. *Let your Goddesses be your guide!*

More Sharing, More Learning, More Fun

Why not give a friend a Goddess Checklist to do and share? Think of all you'll be learning about each other! (Feel free to photocopy for non-commercial use.)

Or...

Live dangerously! give a Chart to your "significant other." Will he dare to "tell it like it is"—like he *really* sees you? If the Seven Goddesses profile he draws of you makes you feel good, here's a playing field for two! But if he's way off, isn't it better to know it now and save time and heartaches for both of you?

Let's have a party—a Goddess Party!

Guests—both women and men—check off a copy of the Goddess Chart. Then the fun begins. Ideas: Guests compare

 Charts in pairs or small groups; C h a r a d e s , guests choose a Goddess to act out while audi- ence tries to guess which one. It's a riot! Goddess decor,  refreshments, and you—"the hostess with the mostess!"

NOTE: Guests do not need the book to participate, but if they desire a copy, before or after, see **deep Goddess Party discount** on order form in back of book.

"Goddess Characteristics": A Checklist. Name_____ Date_____

My age is _____ years. I am:

( ) a woman, describing myself

( ) a man describing ( ) a woman friend

( ) wife

( ) other _____

Directions For Women: Go down the list of all items for all 7 Goddesses and make a check mark in the column after each item that describes you as you are now. If an item does not apply, make no mark.

Directions For Men: have in mind a particular woman and follow directions above, checking to describe the way *you see her now.*

The Goddess Artemis

	√
feels equal to men	
affiliate of women	
strong sense of identity	
activist	
strongly felt causes	
nature lover	
assertive	
independent	
athletic	
men not needed	

The Goddess Athena

men as colleagues	
high achiever	
mature strategist	
cool under fire	
priority: own needs	
authoritative	
confident	
interest in world affairs	
physically active	
chaste	

The Goddess Hestia

spiritual	
non-assertive	
no sense of pressure	
quiet, introspective	
domestic	
orderly housekeeper	
inner centeredness	
loves rituals	
"old soul" presence	
excellent counselor	

- **Tear-out copy in back of book.**
- **Permission to photocopy for personal, non-commercial use hereby granted.**

Copyright © 1985 by Don H. Parker

The Goddess Hera

	√
marriage first, career 2nd	
wife first, mother 2nd	
personal friendships, 2nd	
seeks status symbol life	
heroic in support of mate	
blind to mate's defects	
jealous	
watchful	
radiant when happy	
shrew when betrayed	

The Goddess Demeter

loving	
motherhood paramount	
loves pregnancies	
enjoys serving others	
patient, persevering	
generous	
solid, dependable	
volunteering	
not "ambitious"	
"feminine" jobs	

The Goddess Persephone

extremely feminine	
compliant in nature	
can be "sex-kitten"	
adapts to wishes of others	
likes to be sheltered	
lacks direction	
difficulty following through	
rebellious	
manipulative	
dream oriented	

The Goddess Aphrodite

sensual, passionate	
unconventional	
creative, enthusiastic	
need variety in work	
need variety in men	
"here and now" attitude	
art, music, dance, poetry	
lover of laughter	
wide circle of friends	
not possessive, jealous	

For a closer look...Women: Look over the items under each Goddess again. Are there some characteristics you'd rather have less of? Then draw a line through that item. Like to have some additional qualities you do not now have? Draw a circle around those items. Now look at your "picture." **Men**: Do the same for the woman in your mind, describing how you would like her to be. Now look at her "picture."

Know your goddesses even better.   **Who looks like whom?**
Who says what?

First, look at the picture of each goddess,

Now look at picture No. 1. What are the chief goddess characteristics of this woman? With which goddess does she most closely identify? Write her name under the picture.

Next, put yourself in her place. Ask yourself: "What is she (am I) thinking right now?" Briefly write it underneath.

Artemis

Athena

Hestia

Hera

Demeter

Persephone

Aphrodite

1. _____
      Goddess
I am thinking _____
_____
_____
_____

2. _____
      Goddess
I am thinking _____
_____
_____
_____

3. _____
      Goddess
I am thinking _____
_____
_____
_____

4. _____
      Goddess
I am thinking _____
_____
_____
_____

5. _____
      Goddess
I am thinking _____
_____
_____
_____

6. _____
      Goddess
I am thinking _____
_____
_____
_____

7. _____
      Goddess
I am thinking _____
_____
_____
_____

"Goddess Characteristics": A Checklist. Name_____ Date_____

My age is _____ years. I am:

( ) a woman, describing myself

( ) a man describing ( ) a woman friend

( ) wife

( ) other _____

Directions For Women: Go down the list of all items for all 7 Goddesses and make a check mark in the column after each item that describes you as you are now. If an item does not apply, make no mark.

Directions For Men: have in mind a particular woman and follow directions above, checking to describe the way *you see her now*.

The Goddess Artemis

	√
feels equal to men	
affiliate of women	
strong sense of identity	
activist	
strongly felt causes	
nature lover	
assertive	
independent	
athletic	
men not needed	

The Goddess Athena

men as colleagues	
high achiever	
mature strategist	
cool under fire	
priority: own needs	
authoritative	
confident	
interest in world affairs	
physically active	
chaste	

The Goddess Hestia

spiritual	
non-assertive	
no sense of pressure	
quiet, introspective	
domestic	
orderly housekeeper	
inner centeredness	
loves rituals	
"old soul" presence	
excellent counselor	

- **Tear-out copy in back of book.**
- **Permission to photocopy for personal, non-commercial use hereby granted.**

Copyright © 1985 by Don H. Parker

The Goddess Hera

	√
marriage first, career 2nd	
wife first, mother 2nd	
personal friendships, 2nd	
seeks status symbol life	
heroic in support of mate	
blind to mate's defects	
jealous	
watchful	
radiant when happy	
shrew when betrayed	

The Goddess Demeter

loving	
motherhood paramount	
loves pregnancies	
enjoys serving others	
patient, persevering	
generous	
solid, dependable	
volunteering	
not "ambitious"	
"feminine" jobs	

The Goddess Persephone

extremely feminine	
compliant in nature	
can be "sex-kitten"	
adapts to wishes of others	
likes to be sheltered	
lacks direction	
difficulty following through	
rebellious	
manipulative	
dream oriented	

The Goddess Aphrodite

sensual, passionate	
unconventional	
creative, enthusiastic	
need variety in work	
need variety in men	
"here and now" attitude	
art, music, dance, poetry	
lover of laughter	
wide circle of friends	
not possessive, jealous	

For a closer look...Women: Look over the items under each Goddess again. Are there some characteristics you'd rather have less of? Then draw a line through that item. Like to have some additional qualities you do not now have? Draw a circle around those items. Now look at your "picture." **Men:** Do the same for the woman in your mind, describing how you would like her to be. Now look at her "picture."

Know your goddesses even better.   **Who looks like whom?**
Who says what?

First, look at the picture of each goddess,

Now look at picture No. 1. What are the chief goddess characteristics of this woman? With which goddess does she most closely identify? Write her name under the picture.

Next, put yourself in her place. Ask yourself: "What is she (am I) thinking right now?" Briefly write it underneath.

Artemis

Athena

Hestia

Hera

Demeter

Persephone

Aphrodite

1. _____
   Goddess
   I am thinking _____
   _____
   _____
   _____

2. _____
   Goddess
   I am thinking _____
   _____
   _____
   _____

3. _____
   Goddess
   I am thinking _____
   _____
   _____
   _____

4. _____
   Goddess
   I am thinking _____
   _____
   _____
   _____

5. _____
   Goddess
   I am thinking _____
   _____
   _____
   _____

6. _____
   Goddess
   I am thinking _____
   _____
   _____
   _____

7. _____
   Goddess
   I am thinking _____
   _____
   _____
   _____

44. Exploring–Digging Deeper

You've been "trying them on for size" and probably finding out a lot of new things about yourself. Some surprises? If you really put yourself wholeheartedly into each scenario, you most certainly did!

Perhaps not now, but at some point, you may wish to do more "looking in"—digging deeper into the gold mine that is your very own.

On the next seven pages you will find an extended list of Goddess Characteristics to help you refine and clarify your understanding of what makes you think and act the way you uniquely do. And how others react to you the way they do. The rewards of such exploration will continue to enrich your life and the lives of those around you.

ARTEMIS: *Goddess of Nature; Competitor, Sister*

If you wish to look deeper into the well of your being, check off your favorite characteristics.

	Always	Sometimes	Seldom
I feel . . .			
Equal to men			
Solidarity with sisters			
Sense of purpose			
Inspired to compete			
Need for adventure			
Emotional about nature			
Worried about pollution			
I think . . .			
Modern means frivolous			
Romance is illusion			
Perfume insults nature			
Plastic destroys beauty			
Fairies really live			
Forests are dying			
Health is power			
I do . . .			
Prefer female friends			
Take action now			
Fight for right			
Judge others intensely			
Debate my point			
Protect the earth			
Some mysterious things			
I can be *more* by:			

ATHENA: *Goddess of Wisdom*

If you wish to look deeper into
the well of your being, check off
your favorite characteristics.

I feel . . .	Always	Sometimes	Seldom
Resonance with men			
Satisfaction in work			
Pressure to succeed			
Exhilarated in conflict			
Consumed by power			
Intellectually evolved			
Divinely influenced			
I think . . .			
Strategy creates success			
Achievement proves merit			
Digital improves life			
Computers could rule			
Sleeping wastes time			
Beauty courts power			
Sex distracts from resolve			
I do . . .			
Prefer to lead			
Support my colleagues			
Play to win			
Avoid emotional encounters			
Refuse to cry			
Puzzles, weave, fence			
Excel at chess			
I can be *more* by:			

HESTIA: *Goddess of Hearth and Temple*

If you wish to look deeper into the well of your being, check off your favorite characteristics.

I feel . . .	Always	Sometimes	Seldom
Secretly blessed			
Inner spiritual source			
Fulfilled by loving			
Sense of wholeness			
Harmonious with life			
Absorbed in being			
Ancient knowing			
I think . . .			
Women serve			
Karma is law			
Violence is illness			
Herbs surpass chemicals			
Dancing heals			
Flowers touch the soul			
Music is language			
I do . . .			
Meditation chants			
Love my plants			
Keep a diary			
Inspire cooperation			
Teach yoga			
Cook Thanksgiving dinner			
Need time alone			
I can be *more* by:			

HERA: *Goddess of Marriage*

If you wish to look deeper into the well of your being, check off your favorite characteristics.

I feel . . .	Always	Sometimes	Seldom
Desperate without mate			
Powerful as wife			
Happy when attended			
Threatened by females			
Angry when betrayed			
Vengeful when wronged			
Obsessed with possessions			
I think . . .			
Status represents worth			
Image is everything			
New is better			
Divorce is wrong			
Business trips are dangerous			
Vacations are honeymoons			
Love causes pain			
I do . . .			
Defend my man			
Spend for fun			
Demand respect			
Host business dinners			
Lose control			
Crumble in defeat			
Live with suspicion			
I can be *more* by:			

DEMETER: *Goddess of Grain, Nurturer, Mother*

If you wish to look deeper into
the well of your being, check off
your favorite characteristics.

I feel . . .	Always	Sometimes	Seldom
An urge to reproduce			
Fulfilled as mother			
Useless without children			
Depressed when alone			
Strong as giver			
Need to feed			
Happy when serving			
I think . . .			
Mothers rule world			
Children need protecting			
Women belong home			
Sex is sweet			
Touch is nourishing			
Hot food heals			
Wealth is shared			
I do . . .			
Monitor my children			
Keep neighbors' kids			
Smother those loved			
All the cooking			
Work as nurse			
Contribute to charities			
Teach LaMaze			
I can be *more* by:			

PERSEPHONE: *Goddess of Mystery; Eternal Maiden*

If you wish to look deeper into
the well of your being, check off
your favorite characteristics.

	Always	Sometimes	Seldom
I feel . . .			
Vulnerable to men			
Attracted to power			
Driven by passion			
Angry with rules			
Confused about life			
Happy when playing			
Dominated by dreams			
I think . . .			
Men will provide			
Wealth is security			
Excitement is necessary			
End justifies means			
Mom's the greatest			
Science is magic			
Artists are special			
I do . . .			
Dress for men			
Beg for attention			
Love office parties			
Try everything once			
Blindly jump in			
Follow the leader			
Learn from mistakes			
I can be *more* by:			

APHRODITE: *Goddess of Love, Beauty, and Creativity*

If you wish to look deeper into the well of your being, check off your favorite characteristics.

I feel ...	Always	Sometimes	Seldom
Sensuous seductive powers			
Joyful sexual freedom			
Attracted by eroticism			
Forever "in love"			
Compelled to connect			
Urges to create			
Movement toward change			
I think...			
Joy heals			
Romance feeds the soul			
Flirting suggests acceptance			
Vitality creates beauty			
People are important			
Conformity breeds regret			
Fashion is theater			
I do...			
Strongly influence men			
Project animal magnetism			
Command an audience			
Fill any room			
Celebrate life			
Charm away negatives			
Music, art, dance			
I can be *more* by:			

LET'S CELEBRATE...!!

What a grand scheme!
  —the mountains pushed up,
    the meadows laid flat,
    the seas poured full,

And we, given
  —eyes to see it all,
    ears to hear it all,
    noses to smell it all,
    muscles and skin to feel it all,
    hearts to love it all,
    and a palate to taste

the wine of Life!

—Don Parker

...and so, into the 21st Century with your GODDESS POWER!

HOW TO FIND THE GODDESS GAMES

BIBLIOGRAPHY

Abbott, Franklin, ed. *New Men, New Minds*. Freedom, CA: The Crossing Press, 1987.

A Century of Women (3-cassette video series), 1994, Turner Home Entertainment, Atlanta, Georgia.

Ahsen, Akhter. *Aphrodite, The Psychology of Consciousness*. New York: Brandon House, Inc., 1988.

Alther, Lisa. *Other Women*. New York: New American Library, August, 1985.

Andrews, Lynn V. *Jaguar Woman*. New York: Harper & Row, Publishers, Inc., 1985.

Apple, Max. "My First Girlfriend", *Esquire*, New York, June, 1986, p. 123.

Aslett, Don. *Who Says It's A Woman's Job To Clean*. Cincinnati, Ohio: Writer's Digest Books, 1986.

Barbach, Lonnie, Ph.D., ed. *Pleasures*. Garden City, New York: Doubleday & Company, Inc., 1984.

Becker, Carol. *The Invisible Drama, Women And The Anxiety Of Change,* New York: MacMillan Publishing, 1987.

Beilenson, Evelyn L. and Ann Tenenbaum. *Wit and Wisdom of Famous American Women*. White Plains, New York: Peter Pauper Press, Inc., 1986.

Blotnick, Srully, Dr. *Otherwise Engaged*. New York: Facts On File Publications, 1985.

Blum, Arlene. *Annapurna, A Woman's Place*. San Francisco: Sierra Club Books, 1980.

Bly, Robert, and Deborah Tannen, In Conversation, "Where Are Women and Men Today?", *New Age Journal,* February,1992, pp. 28-33, 92-97.

Bolen, Jean Shinoda, M.D. *Crossing To Avalon*. San Francisco: HarperSan Francisco, 1994.

——— *Goddesses In Everywoman*. San Francisco: Harper & Row Publishers, 1989.

———— *Goddesses in Everyman*. San Francisco: Harper & Row Publishers, 1987.

Bolles, Richard Nelson. *The 1989 What Color Is Your Parachute?* Berkeley, CA: Ten Speed Press, 1989.

Bradley, Marion Zimmer. *The Mists of Avalon*. New York: Ballantine Books, 1982.

Brandt, Anthony. "Father Love", *Esquire*. November 1982, pp. 8, 81-89.

Brownmiller, Susan. *Femininity*. New York: Fawcett Columbine, 1984.

Budapest, Z. "A Witch's Manifesto", *Whole Earth Review,* No. 74. Spring 1992, pp. 34-42.

———— *The Goddess In The Office,* San Francisco: HarperSanFrancisco, 1993.

———— *The Goddess In The Bedroom,* San Francisco: HarperSanFrancisco, 1995.

Campbell, Joseph. *The Masks Of God: Creative Mythology*. New York: Penguin Books, 1976.

———— *The Power Of Myth With Bill Moyers* (Videocassette Set, Programs 1-6), New York: Apostrophe 8 Productions in association with Public Affairs Television and Alvin A. Perlmutter, Inc., 1988.

Campbell, Susan M. *Beyond The Power Struggle*. San Luis Obispo, CA: Impact Publishers, 1984.

Carlson, Margaret. "Less Than Uplifting", *Time,* April 4, 1994, p. 31.

Carter, Betsy. "Liberation's Next Wave, According To Gloria Steinem", *Esquire*, June, 1984, pp. 202-206.

Chernin, Kim. *The Obsession*. New York: Harper & Row Publishers, 1981.

Christ, Carol P. *Laughter Of Aphrodite*. San Francisco: Harper & Row Publishers, 1987.

Cowan, Dr. Connell and Kinder, Dr. Melvin. *Smart Women, Foolish Choices*. New York: Clarkson N. Potter, Inc.,

1985.

Davis, Elizabeth Gould. *The First Sex*. Baltimore, Maryland: Penguin Books, Inc., 1971.

Doss, Martha Merrill, ed. *The Directory of Special Opportunities For Women*. Garrett Park, Maryland: Garrett Park Press, 1981.

Downing, Christine. *The Goddesses*. New York: The Crossroad Publishing Company, 1981.

Ehrenreich, Barbara. "The Male Revolt", *Mother Jones*, April 1983, pp. 25-42.

Eisler, Riane. *The Chalice & The Blade*. San Francisco: Harper & Row Publishers, 1987.

———— *Sacred Pleasure*. San Francisco: HarperSanFrancisco, 1995.

Everitt, David and Harold Schechter. *The Manly Handbook*. New York: Berkeley Books, July 1982.

Faludi, Susan and Steinem, Gloria, "Fighting the Backlash Against Feminism", *Time*, March 9, 1992, pp.50-57.

Feinstein, David, Ph.D., Krippner, Stanley, Ph.D. *Personal Mythology*. Los Angeles: Jeremy P. Tarcher, Inc., 1988.

Feldman, Edmund Burke. *Art As Image And Idea*. Englewood Cliffs, New Jersey: Prentice-Hall, Inc., 1967.

Ferguson, Marilyn. *The Aquarian Conspiracy*. Los Angeles: J.P. Tarcher, Inc. 1980.

Firestone, Ross, Ed. *A Book Of Men*. New York: Stonehill Publishing Company, 1978.

Forward, Susan, Dr. and Joan Torres. *Men Who Hate Women And The Women Who Love Them*. New York: Bantam Books, 1986.

Fried, Stephen. "A Night Out With The Boys", *San Francisco Chronicle*, January 18, 1987, This World, pp.7-12.

Friedan, Betty. *The Feminine Mystique*. New York: Dell Publishing Co., Inc. 1983.

——— *The Second Stage*. New York: Summit Books, 1981.

Friedman, Sonya. *Smart Cookies Don't Crumble*. New York: G.P. Putnam's Sons, 1985.

Gadon, Elinor W. *The Once & Future Goddess*. San Francisco: HarperSanFrancisco, 1989.

Gould, Roger L., M.D., *Transformations*. New York: Simon and Schuster, 1978.

Gray, John, Ph.D. *Men Are From Mars, Women Are From Venus*. New York: HarperCollins Publishers, 1992.

Green, Blake. "Goddess Worship In The 80's", *San Francisco Chronicle*, March 21, 1987, People, p. 13.

Grimal, Pierre. *The Dictionary Of Classical Mythology*. New York: Basil Blackwell, Inc., 1986.

Guttentag, Marcia and Paul F. Secord. *Too Many Women?* Beverly Hills, CA: Sage Publications, Inc. 1983.

Jackson, Donna. *How To Make The World A Better Place For Women In Five Minutes A Day*. New York: Hyperion, 1992.

Jeffers, Susan, Ph.D., *Opening Our Hearts To Men*. New York: Ballantine Books, 1989.

Jiggins, Janice. *Changing the Boundaries*. Washington, DC: Island Press, 1994.

Johnson, Robert A. *She, Understanding Feminine Psychology*. New York: Harper & Row, Publishers, 1976.

——— *He, Understanding Masculine Psychology*. New York: Harper & Row, Publishers, 1977.

——— *We: Understanding the Psychology of Romantic Love*. San Francisco: Harper & Row, Publishers, 1983.

Jung, C. G. *Memories, Dreams, Reflections*. New York: Vintage Books, 1965.

Keating, Kathleen. *Hug Therapy 2*. Minneapolis: Comp Care Publishers, 1987.

Keen, Sam. *Fire In The Belly, On Being A Man*. New York: Bantam Books, 1991.

───── *The Passionate Life Stages Of Loving*. San Francisco: Harper and Row, Publishers, 1983.

Keeton, Kathy and Baskin, Yvonne. *Woman of Tomorrow*. New York: St. Martin's/Marek, 1985.

Keuls, Eva C. *The Reign of the Phallus*. New York: Harper & Row, Publishers, 1985.

Koch, Rudolf. *The Book Of Signs*. English translation first published by the First Edition Club of London, 1930. Reprint, New York: Dover Publications, n.d.

Leeming, David and Page, Jake. *Goddess, Myths of The Female Divine*. New York: Oxford University Press, 1994.

Leonard, George. "The End of Sex", *Esquire*, December 1982, pp. 70-80.

Leonard, Linda Schierse. *The Wounded Woman*. Boston: Shambhala Publications, Inc., 1983.

Lerner, Gerda. *The Creation of Patriarchy*. New York: Oxford University Press, 1986.

Levinson, Daniel J. *The Seasons Of A Man's Life*. New York: Stonehill Publishing Company, 1978.

Lovelock, J.E., *Gaia*. New York: Oxford University Press, 1979.

Markale, Jean. *Women Of The Celts*. Rochester, Vermont: Inner Traditions International, Ltd., 1975.

Martz, Sandra Haldeman. *I Am becoming The Woman I've Wanted*. Watsonville, CA: Papier-Mache Press, 1994.

Masuda, Yoneji. *The Information Society As Post-Industrial Society*. Bethesda, Maryland: World Future Society, 1981.

McCoy, Vivian Rogers; Ryan, Colleen; Sutton, Robin; Winn, Nancy. *A Life Transition's Reader*. Lawrence, Kansas: The University of Kansas, 1980.

Mervin, Sabrina and Prunhuber, Carol. *Women Around The World And Through The Ages.* Wilmington, DE: Atomium Books, 1990.

Moffitt, Phillip, "Sex And Friendship", *Esquire*, December 1982, p.9.

Montagu, Ashley. *The Natural Superiority Of Women.* New York: MacMillan Publishing Co., 1974.

Morgan, Elaine. *The Descent of Woman.* New York: Stein and Day, 1985.

New Larousse Encyclopedia Of Mythology. New York: Prometheus Press, 1968.

Nicholson, Joanna, *How To Be Sexy Without Looking Sleazy.* Manassas Park, VA: Impact Publications, 1995.

———— "The Way To Be Surely, Surely Sexy", *Cosmopolitan*, February, 1995, p. 80.

Norwood, Robin. *Women Who Love Too Much.* Los Angeles: Jeremy P. Tarcher, Inc., 1985.

Nudel, Adele. *For The Woman Over 50.* New York: Avon Books, 1978.

O'Faolain and Martines, Lauro, ed. *Not In God's Image.* New York: Harper & Row, Publishers, Inc., 1973.

Okely, Judith. *Simone DeBeauvoir.* New York: Pantheon Books, 1986.

Parry, Danaan and Lila Forest. *The Earthsteward's Handbook.* Cooperstown, NY: Sunstone Publications, 1991.

———— *Essene Book of Meditations.* Cooperstown, NY: Sunstone Publications, 1991.

Perper, Timothy. *Sex Signals.* Philadelphia: ISI Press, 1985.

Pietropinto, Anthony, M.D., and Jacqueline Simenauer. *Beyond The Male Myth.* New York: Times Books, 1977.

Pomeroy, Sarah B. *Goddesses, Whores, Wives, and Slaves.* New York: Schoken Books, 1975.

Prasinos, Steven and Tittler, Bennett I. "Love Styles", *Journal of Humanistic Psychology*, Vol. 24, No. 1, p.175.

Randall, Michael H. "Do Tabloids Turn Housewives Into Zombies?", *Whole Earth Review*, No. 52, Fall 1986, pp. 93-95.

Read, Donna. *Women and Spirituality* (Videocassette Trilogy), Montreal, Canada, in cooperation with the National Film Board of Canada, 1990.

Robinson, Charles Alexander, Jr. *An Anthology of Greek Drama*. New York: Holt, Rinehart and Winston, Inc., 1949.

Rogers, Natalie. *Emerging Woman*. Point Reyes, CA: Personal Press, 1980.

Satterthwaite, Frank. "Men Competing With Women", *Esquire*, May 1983, pp. 101-104.

Sears, Robert R. and Shirley S.Feldman, ed. *The Seven Ages Of Man*. Los Altos, CA: William Kaufmann, Inc., 1964.

Shapiro, Stephen A. *Manhood*. New York: G.P. Putnam's Sons, 1984.

Shaver, Philip and Clyde Hendrick. *Sex and Gender*. Newbury Park, CA: Sage Publications, Inc., 1987.

Sheehy, Gail. *Passages*. New York: Bantam Books, June, 1977.

Shepherd, Linda Jean. Lifting the Veil: *The Feminine Face of Science*. Boston: Shambhala Publications, Inc., 1993.

Shiva, Vandana. *Close To Home (Women Reconnect Ecology, Health and Development Worldwide)*. Philadelphia: New Society Publishers, 1994.

Sommers, Christina Hoff. *Who Stole Feminism*. New York: Simon and Schuster, 1994.

Steinem, Gloria. *Outrageous Acts And Everyday Rebellions*. New York: New American Library, January, 1986.

Stone, Merlin. *When God Was A Woman*. New York: Harcourt

Brace Jovanovich, Publishers, 1976.

———— *Ancient Mirrors Of Womanhood*. Boston: Beacon Press, 1984.

Stromberg, Ann H., Laurie Larwood and Barbara A. Gutek, ed. *Women and Work, Volume 2*. Newbury Park, CA: Sage Publications, Inc., 1987.

Suleiman, Susan Rubin, ed. *The Female Body In Western Culture*. Cambridge, Massachusetts: Harvard University Press, 1986.

Swain, Sally. *Oh My Goddess!* New York: Penguin Books, 1994.

Theobald, Robert. *Beyond Despair*. Washington, DC: Seven Locks Press, Inc., 1976.

Vaillant, George E. "How The Best And The Brightest Came Of Age", *Psychology Today*. September 1977, pp. 34-41.

Walker, Barbara. *The Woman's Encyclopedia of Myths and Secrets*. San Francisco: Harper & Row, Publishers, 1983.

Waring, Richard, ed. *Zone, A Feminist Journal For Women And Men*, 1988.

Wells, Diana. (compiled). *Getting There, The Movement Toward Gender Equality*. New York: Carroll & Graf Publishers/Richard Gallen, 1994.

Westheimer, Ruth. *Dr. Ruth's Guide For Married Lovers*. New York: Warner Books, 1986.

Witkin-Lanoil, Georgia, Ph.D. *The Female Stress Syndrome*. New York: New Market Press, 1984.

———— *The Male Stress Syndrome*. New York: Newmarket Press, 1986.

Woolger, Jennifer Barker and J. Roger. *The Goddess Within*. New York: Ballantine Books, 1987.

Index

The author soaking up Goddess Power on the Acropolis
overlooking Athens. Here we see the caryatids supporting one wing of the Erechtheum, built and dedicated to
Goddess Athena circa 410 B.C.

Special Psy-Plan Discount

for

- Group leaders
- Workshop presenters
- Therapists, counselors

"An expanding array of group techniques are becoming potent, affordable remedies, even for medical problems.... Psychologists and other mental health professionals are creating group therapy approaches for a host of medical conditions as well as for mental disorders and psychosocial problems."*

Dear Professional:

I have designed the book, *Goddess Power*, from nearly a half-century of work in the psychology of learning, individual differences, individual counseling and as a workshop presenter. You will find that the one-page Goddess Characteristic Chart alone gives rapid and effective access to the currently operative psychosocial energies employed by the individual in daily living. From the emerging pattern of motivation, the book proceeds to deepen insights becoming a tool for creative cooperative problem solving in the hands of both counselee and counselor.

Don H. Parker, Ph.D., APA Member since 1958

*The Monitor, American Psychological Association, Vol. 26, July 1995, front page.

Call *toll-free*
1-800-BOOKLOG (266-5564)
24 hours a day, every day

Ask for "Psy-Plan"

Order Form
(Tear out or photocopy)

If you are unable to locate additional copies of this book in your bookstore, you may call *toll-free*

1-800-BOOKLOG (266-5564)
24 hours a day, every day

We accept Visa or MasterCard, or order from

Dynamic Publishing BK
148 San Remo Road
Carmel, CA 93923

Please print your name and address or gift name and address. Please ship my book(s) to:

Name_____

Street_____

City_____ State_____Zip_____

I am enclosing $24.95 (please add $3.00 to cover shipping and handling. California residents add an additional $1.93 sales tax; New Jersey residents add $1.50 sales tax). Send check or money order made payable to DYNAMIC PUBLISHING. Please do not send cash. No CODs.

Total Amount Enclosed $_____.___

Goddess Party Orders — *15% Discount*

on all Goddess Party orders of 3 or more books sent to one address. Please enclose $21.20 per book (add $1.50 per book to cover shipping and handling. California residents add an additional $1.64 per book sales tax; New Jersey residents add $1.27 per book sales tax). Send check or money order made payable to DYNAMIC PUBLISHING. Please do not send cash. No CODs.

Total Amount Enclosed $ _____.___

Or call TOLL FREE 1-800-BOOKLOG (266-5564)

Bookstore Quanity Discount 1-800-879-4214